THE GUIDE TO DATING FOR THE
MATURE WOMAN
USING THE DATING SITES

(HOW I GOT MY MAN)

DR. FERRIS E. MERHISH
AND MARY MERHISH

authorHOUSE

AuthorHouse™
1663 Liberty Drive
Bloomington, IN 47403
www.authorhouse.com
Phone: 833-262-8899

Published by AuthorHouse 03/04/2022

ISBN: 978-1-6655-5393-3 (sc)
ISBN: 978-1-6655-5391-9 (hc)
ISBN: 978-1-6655-5392-6 (e)

Library of Congress Control Number: 2022904230

I am dedicating this book to my wives and the relationships I had with them. I lost my first wife after being in a relationship with her for over twenty-eight years, and finally we broke up after about thirty years. Now, for most of the time, I believed that we had a good relationship, but things started to go south around the twenty-seventh year. I lost my second wife three and a half years ago to two cancers; we seemed to beat breast cancer, but liver cancer took her. We were together for nearly twenty-three years, and she came to me because of a long and unforeseen breakup with my first wife. I have to say she was a very surprising blessing, and not only did she bring love to my heart and romance back into my like, but she was truly instrumental in helping me recover from a difficult situation, an economic person disaster because of the separation and divorce from my first wife, and untimely the collapse my career. With her help, I was able to recover and more.

I must say I am very grateful for finding my current fiancée. I met her during the research and writing of this book. Not only has she been an inspiration, but she helps me recover from my depression from my loss. She is hardworking, independent, fair, loving, and supporting. She has helped me with my fourth book about dating issues and ideas, which I did for men, as well as this one for women. She has offered some of her perspectives from the women's point of view. I hope you will find this valuable as you pursue that special person.

CONTENTS

INTRODUCTION

We find ourselves using dating sites for many reasons, and we need to agree that in many ways, we are in the same boat. I am going to share with you my experiences and views, looking at them from the perspective of a man, and not just my own perspective. I have also talked to other men. I believe this is going to be a benefit to you, because I am going to try to give you information that you can use, based on not being filtered by a woman. If you think we think differently, you may have a shoe up on other gals (and of course many men). I must admit here that the work I am doing in both these books will not always sit well with you gals sometimes, but for the gentleman who I hope buys this book, I hope we are close. But you can know my swing here as you use the book as a guide to find that new special person, be it a friend or a significant other.

We each have our reasons for turning to something that might give us some guidance and solve one of our life's problems. For me, it was overwhelming. I am sure a great many of you can understand and identify with my needs, wants, and losses. We are all flesh and blood. When we hurt, we cry in pain; if we get cut, we bleed. When we lose someone, we deeply love. Don't we hurt with deep pain to the bottom of our souls? Well, I lost my second wife, and I had deep love for her during and after battle with two cancers. I recently told her daughter that when we met, as far as I was concerned, we never looked back. I was deeply in love with her. We were married very quickly and were together for about twenty-three years.

I have been an educator, businessman, entrepreneur, technician in aerospace for a major missile and space firm, and in the later years an author and marketing guy. Yes, I was married before, for nearly 30 years. And yes, I loved her and chased her all over the San Jose, California, area. She was a virgin and the mother of my two grown children. She was a schoolteacher—and very good, I may add—and she helped me reach one of my dreams.

I would often spend time helping her after school in her classroom, and she helped me as a new beginning teacher, and with the many issues of going back to college to earn my degrees.

The truth is I never for a moment got hung up on the virgin part. The love bug hit me, and really this is all I thought about. I wanted to marry her and ride off into the sunset. Also, after serving in the navy for not quite four years, I wanted more out of life, and I believed that going to college was the avenue for doing this. I still believe this is true, and I can see where making this sacrifice paid off, but there was a cost too. So in talking to her about our future together, I asked her to help me go to college. She agreed and said, "I would like to have children." This was not on my agenda at the time, but we both agreed. Today, yes, I would like to have more kids. Maybe in my next book, I will share with you why I had a change of heart.

Bobbie, my second wife, and I were different. I never thought about it at the time, but as I said to many of my friends, we never looked back, we were married in three months. I believe I was fifty-six, and she was fifty-two. Her two daughters were nearly grown-up, one a little older and more squared away then the other, but the younger daughter turned around very nicely. And yes, I would like to see her more, but she is out of state, and we were not as close as I was with the older daughter. I believe we are still closer than I am with my own kids. As much as she was willing to allow me, I was able to take her under my wing. I have gotten close with the oldest, Bri, and her husband is very close to me—in fact, closer to me than my own two children. I am not happy in many ways about this, but this is where it is, and I am working on it.

We did not talk about having children much, to tell the truth, and I couldn't have kids anyway. I am not sure about her, but I gave up on this privilege. As I said, I lost Bobbie to two cancers. I saw her pass away, and she was taken from me. Oh, yes, I started to fall apart. A couple of my friends saw this and encouraged me to write again. At the time, I had been away from writing for some time. I had written three career and vocational books, but I had been away from being an author for years. Bobbie had asked me to stop writing before we moved to Texas, and I did. Now, here I was going into a depression, with up to four depression pains a day.

But these two friends of mine, Vern Thomason and Jack Worthington, got after me. Both were old friends, and I would really like to see them more, but we talked on the phone and via e-mail often. It is not the same thing.

I said to Vern and Jack, "I have no idea what to write about." Then it hit me. I had one book on the market, and now there is this one. This one is for you, gals. I am trying to give something back that will help all of us.

As you are aware, we have many reasons why we might want to find help finding a new companion, serious friend, pal, traveling partner, or lover. You may have gotten out of the dating circle, become a widow, or divorced. I was out of the dating circle. You may not have the time now as you did before, or you don't know where to go, or you are not interested in going to places by yourself. We all have various motivations. I didn't know where to go and was lost in many ways. This was new territory for me. I came from California, I was married for twenty-three years, and I didn't go to bars.

Does this sound like you? You don't have to be exactly like me, but we all can be out of this loop. As I said, I am not a bar guy, I don't really drink, and I don't smoke. This kept me away from obvious hangout spots. Sure, I know they have changed the rules, but many places still smell anyway, and it is very noisy for me. And if you really want to know, I was off the depression pills also, so I was home with my dogs watching TV most of the time. Where were you?

Now, understand I have not used all the sites in the development of my work here, but I was on four, using some more than others. I also sought experience from others like you guys and gals. I have been talking, writing, meeting, dating, and communicating with a good number of you gals. I had to find a new mate three times, and to tell the truth, I was seriously dating before I met my first wife. The first time was not the first time at all, but I am leaving this experience out. I was a younger guy, and we dated for only a while, but the parents pushed us to not marry twice, so I backed out the second time and got the ring back. My experience with my first wife was similar but still different; it seemed easier and faster too.

Now, I have not used dating sites at all, so you may find your experience different from mine, and there are different perspectives: you are women, and I am a seventy-nine-year-old man with a PhD. I am six foot three, have most of my own hair, was in several branches of the military, and have been in several industries. I taught in several colleges, graduate schools, and education systems in two states and China, so I have some experience working with a lot of people at various levels. I had two of my own businesses and worked for several large firms.

We have all faced many problems, but differently. We all put our pants on one leg at a time. I am sure there are some of you who may jump into them with both legs at the same time, but I don't. I am not going to address you gal participants regarding quality because beauty is in the eyes of the beholder. As an example, in my dating process, I can look at and have at another participant, and bang—I have made an instant judgment, or the gal I would like to talk to does this too. By the end of your meeting, you may have come to a conclusion that is right or wrong, but it is how you feel. So I am going to present my male view, offering my view and critics related to challenges, disappointments, and frustrations one might go through trying to find a gentleman, boyfriend, lover, or pal of your choice. However, I am not going to try to convince you that this represents all male perspectives.

One way or another, I met, talked on the phone, e-mailed, talked in person, and went out with a number of women. Some liked me, some I liked, and there were many who would have anything to do with me because I was not of the same political party, I belong to the NRA and like and use firearms, or I hunt wild pigs. I was now looking for someone who had similar views as I did at the time, and I wanted to find a nice gal to go to the range with. No, this wasn't something I had to do all the time, because I also liked movies, plays, nice dinners, the fair, and more. But it would be fun to enjoy some of the same views too. I talked to one nice-sounding and nice-looking woman, but she said to me, "If you are not a Democrat, I am not interested." I don't care if you are a Democrat or Republican because I have been both. I kind of vote for the idea, or what the individual has to say or stands for. I have found that these politicians may say one thing and do something else. Anyway this is where I come from, and I would expect that many of you may think the same way. Oh, I liked Ike, but I also liked Harry Truman, and I voted for Ronald Ragan and John Kennedy. I was not old enough to vote for Harry or Ike, but I might have. I used to ride horses, but I am not sure if I still can. What I am getting at is I have changed—we all do. I used to have a crew cut, and now I have longer hair, but it is not as black as it used to be. I don't run as fast or walk as far either.

Then one day, I met a gal at the gun club, and we often met and shot at an indoor range, but she was married, so this didn't develop. Along the way, with my research, I met a gal who also liked to go to movies and plays. We started to go to the gun range, and she enjoyed shooting. We both had licenses to carry. I started to train her, and then we started to get serious. I had been dating another nice gal, and I met her family, but she lived in Dallas, about fifty miles from where I was living, so I broke it off. But then I found out that this new woman who enjoyed a number of things I did also lived in Dallas. I continued to see her, we dated more and more, and soon I was dating her full time and as often as I could. I even purchased her a handgun, and today she is my fiancée.

I am going to assume that a good number tried hanging out at a bar or club. How is this working out for you? I am not going to attack this, but personally I am not too sure this is a good trend. I never did too well trying to date this way. First, to be fair, I couldn't handle the smoke, and I wasn't much of a drinker. I am going to assume there is a stigma associated with this to some degree. But I must admit looking for someone special online is better than the club. Of course, this is my opinion, and using one or more dating services has worked for me. Over the years, I have used the system. The process has matured a lot, but the bottom line is the service helps us. Yes, us. I have been involved twice, using it not as a game but as a tool to help me find some companionship, love, and more. At the same time, the experience has invited some negative occurrences and untrustworthy people, as well as persons who are looking to prey on honest individuals looking for love and new beginnings. But yes, I would use the sites again, though maybe different sites to get closer to my needs and wants.

Looking back, as a young man just out of the navy, I did have some success with meeting a few gals in a club. I went to the one near my place in

Sunnyvale, California, as well as a bowling alley in Cupertino. But to tell the truth, I was never a drinker, and I didn't have positive feelings about smoking. I lost my mom and dad to smoking, so I have a little history there.

One thing I would like to point out is that it is dark in these bars, and I suggest you frequent a place where the woman-to-man ratio is more in your favor and not one hundred women for every available man in the world. Here is the thing: you can take this advice or leave it. But as I have told the guys, you need to look at your assets that you are bringing to the playing field and do your best to improve them. Put that smile on, as well as a little polish on your chrome (your nails). Color and comb your hair. And please think about this: Where did we come up with these statistics? Not counting illness, some of our finest young men do not live as long, as much as eight years fewer than women. And I think you will have to agree with me here that wars have taken their toll. Many men are broken, worn-out, and gone mentally.

I missed the wars and battles, but I served in the navy, air force reserves, National Guard, and more. I have been blown down a flight deck on an aircraft carrier, and I have poor hearing from my military experience. I don't know about today, but back when I was working on the flight deck, we had to check the pressure gauge of a running jet engine by going inside the plane as it was running, before it was launched. I am not a perfect candidate either. So right or wrong, these one hundred women that are said to be available for every man in the current world could be your competition. And if you have some doubt about my suggestion, just check your boyfriend's or dad's computer. These offers are coming from all over the world—Japan, South America, Russia, your neighborhood, and more.

So be like us guys when we are taking our cars to show them off. We added some new chrome, put more power under the hood, added new leather inside the vehicle, and got a new paint job or new tires. Is that not any more special than you are? You need to do the same to and for yourself. Get a new snappy dress, change your perfume, and upgrade. Maybe get a new color for your hair, buy shoes, and get a tan. Now, ladies, you are not going to get off that easy. Get your nails done because it is time to turn the page. Go work out at a gym and become a new you, and you may like the new you and what you see!

Yes, men are in short supply, so if you want to catch the biggest and best fish, what do you need? The best bait and the finest lure you can get.

Maybe more qualified ones are in even shorter supply and harder to find. I know that you have seen many movies where the main female actress has on the sharpest dress with nice hair and the biggest smile. At the end of the day, what are you trying to do? You really need to ask yourself this. If he is worth meeting or going after, isn't he worth doing something special for? You are really doing it for the both of you, not just him. Even in the creature world, bugs dance, birds prance around, and some bring gifts. You may feel better by making changes. And change that nineteenth-century perfume. Don't come looking like you slept in the only dress you have. Yes, I met this gal, and when it came to the end of the date, I tried nicely to tell her I wasn't interested in dating her again. This wasn't easy to do, nor is it easy to be rejected. But she came to our first meeting in a "black" dress that looked as if she slept in it or was loaned to her by her witch sister.

I believe that one advantage of being ex-military is they were big on us being clean. I must tell you that I still shower two to three times a day, and for sure if I have a date, I believe it is my responsibility to do this. Sure, I can live out of a box with several other trained sailors, and when I was in the navy, sometimes we had to shower in saltwater that was cold, but we were clean. The new navy, with better technology, has all the hot water they need. I am not in the military anymore, and I am not required to live out of a box or take saltwater showers, but I developed this habit and still do it today.

I do have this man in his fifties who works for me part time, and he seems to be very giving. I talked to him the other day and said, "Larry, I know you help out your kids." He has two older boys and a daughter. In this case, he helps children, but they do little for him. I said, "Why don't you help yourself? You would look and feel better?" This would be true for you, ladies. Lose weight possibly? In Larry's case, this would make him look and feel better, and it would help you too. Raise both of your self-esteem. He also needs work done on his front teeth. I am not sure if he knows that they have this new tool for men called a razor. It has been reported that in the United States today, more than 50 percent of the adult population is overweight, so even if you don't find that guy, you are going to look and feel better anyway. And another point: maybe guys would be more interested in you too. I am sorry if I hurt your feelings somewhat, but it is my job with this book to help you find that special person. But is this easy? No. I know myself. I needed to lose twenty extra pounds, and I worked on it. I was at the doctor's office recently, and I had been working out a little. The nurse told me I had lost about twenty pounds, and just hearing this made me feel better. So you are not doing this for him—it is for you.

My point is it is the responsibility of both people to try to put their best foot forward and to be seen in the best possible light.

I suspect there are other things you can do. As an example, I find that I am a little vain, so I will tell you a secret about me: I dye my hair a little. I know some of you do this too, but there are a few more things you might consider. Have it styled, cut, and so forth. Now, most of you may have your nails done, but you do not necessarily do this for some guy—you are doing it for yourself. I do it for me. Yes, this is like putting a new coat of paint on your kitchen wall to brighten things up a bit. I went to my podiatrist—yes, I am a diabetic too, but I have been having my feet done for some time because it feels good and is healthy. My doctor said that my feet look good. I used to go with my second wife all the time, and now I go with my new gal. It is kind of fun to go together, and we go out to lunch afterward.

Yes, many guys notice women who smoke, but now this is kind of a touchy area. So where in your profile are you going to talk a little about not doing this or that? Drugs and smoking are usually touched on, often before you get together, so it is my opinion that this issue is resolved before you get the meeting or first date. My advice is if you smoke, you will need to run this concept by the person you are going to meet. I would suggest not smoking, but this can be discussed with your new acquaintance. You may not know this, but as a nonsmoker I can smell it on you clothing, hair, and in your car, it permeates everything. So if you are a smoker and can't or don't want to quit, then you need to make this known. I can't speak for other guys, but I really don't want to have a serious relationship with a smoker—or a causal relationship for that matter.

There are two more things I would like to touch base with you on. First, if you have missing teeth, especially up front, yes, it is pricey to fix, but get it permanently put back in. This is something that can often be repaired, and it makes a very big impression on your newfound friend. Don't play with the hole. A few months ago, I went out with a gal, and she took out this plate holding one or more teeth. It was a turnoff for me, and I am going to guess for you too. I don't know about your next date, but a gaping hole would be a turnoff too.

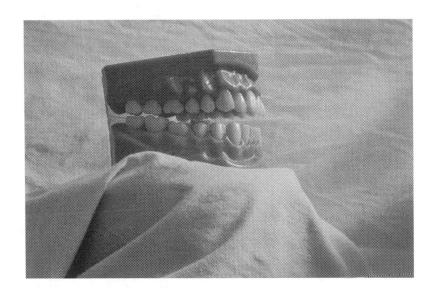

There is one very important area that can shoot you down, and this needs to be resolved by you here and now. As women get older, they seem to find alternatives to being with a man or companion to avoid being lonely. For younger women, maybe not so much. What we start to see here is a shift from wanting male companionship, and they fill this need with the willingness to help take care of their grandchildren. They join card groups, charity organizations, and clubs. They even get a job, play golf or pickleball, volunteer, or travel with girlfriends and families. One can understand this to a point. But it seems that they don't understand when they decide they want the companionship of a gentleman, they need to give up some of those activities because he is going to want to spend time with them. This cuts both ways, but I believe guys have an easier time making this transition. Often this means you need to be willing to give up some activities. Yes, it is hard to give up time with your cute grandkids, that job, or that team commitment. This is understandable. Your new gentleman may want to see you a few times a week, take a weekend cruise with you, or come over a few nights a week. He may want to see a football game, go to a movie, or have you over to his place. There could be day trips or weekend trips. I have a new gal friend, and we are facing this situation ourselves. The truth is I don't want to put too much pressure on her, but I would be willing to give up some of my activities. I don't have many, but I do have one to two activities. I shoot at a local gun club. I used to do this a few times per week, as well as some tactical training once or twice a week. Now, I am trying to include her to be involved with me, or I simply don't go. I am not as tied to my friends, family, and other activities as she is, and it is easier for me, but this may end up in a deal breaker for some couples. I am flexible, but I am not sure how far I can flex. I have talked about living together a few nights and days a week to see how compatible we might be. This isn't *The Adventures of Ozzie and Harriet* here.

Before you are faced with this situation in real life and are required to make a major life-changing situation, start thinking about this need and requirement for the both of you. You must think with both your head and heart. Yes, it is going to take some adjustment on both your parts, and you will have to select some alternatives and solutions. You should be able to make the best choice for yourself, your family, and of course your new acquaintance and relationship.

Like you, men more than likely have one or more outside activities they might like to do, and they may have family to spend time with. Therefore, you now must be more flexible at some point. Again, if you start thinking about these things now, you will be able to make the transition more easily and with less embarrassment.

As I and my girlfriend talked, and as we were working on my first book about dating sites, we were at this point, and she was reading in this area here. She said, "That's me!"

I said to her, "Honey, that is not you. This is hundreds of women across the country."

She asked me, "Well, what are we going to do when I want to go play bridge or pickleball?"

I said, "You go, and I will go shooting at the gun range, or I will stay home and watch TV. I will find something to do."

The Sites and Getting Started

Let's get started looking at the sites. There are several levels of sites to select from, but I am not recommending in any order. To tell the truth, I didn't realize how many there are and that some are more specialized than others. There are also varying costs to joining, and based on what they suggest and do for you, that can increase the cost quite a bit. You need to check this out for yourself and check your budget too. Also, you need to determine not only what you are looking for but how much time you are going to spend on it. Another important thing is how much you are willing to spend.

I suggest that before you get started, you do some soul-searching and make sure this is really something you really want to do. We are about to start playing with other people's hearts and minds, and this is not a game or project one should be taking very lightly. These people are there because in most cases, they want to meet a special person to fill a need that they have, not to play some little dating game. I assure you I was seriously looking for someone to fill my heart and hoping that I could find her. After some time, I did find her, and I suggest that there are many gals and guys out there who feel the same way I did and are out there looking. They could be the people you are looking for.

- **The Christian dating site**
  I am going to believe that most of the participants are just that, Christians. But from my limited experiences dealing with these sites, it is best not to totally assume anything. I hate being a pessimist, but it is better to be safe than sorry.

- **Silver Dating Site (Over fifty)**
  I have found this site to be active in providing a lot of candidates. Often I found that the distance of some of the candidates was too far to reasonably try to date, but now that's just me.

- **Eharmony.com**

  I found this site to be very good in presenting a favorable number of candidates to meet.

- **Mate1.com**

  I have not used this site.

- **Match.com**

  I have not used this site.

- **OurTime**

  I found this one not too bad. Again, the biggest issue was the distance of some of the applicants. I found a lot of interesting women, but in most cases, there were more than one hundred miles between them and me.

- **Zooks Seniors**

  Yes, I have used this site, and here again I found this site to provide me with several candidates, but again many were out of my driving range. Depending on your geographical area, this may or may not be true for you.

You can go on the Internet and find various reviews for each site, as well as what each site claims is best at providing candidates.

Let me say this before you put your money up for a site. Understand what each site is suggesting it is going to provide. Some sites will pride themselves on providing carefully made matches, whereas others have extensive search tools.

I currently have used four of these sites, and if I continue to do research or search for that special gal, I am going to do more research on the site itself before putting up my hard-earned money. I must admit that I didn't go into this search as wise as I should have been.

There are some sites that you don't want to touch with a ten-foot pole, and if you click on them, it can be hard to get rid of them. I shared this same information with the guys. This is simply an ounce of prevention. If you get hooked up with any of them, it might take hours or weeks to get unhooked.

There are a good number of honest men out there, as there are women, seeking a viable relationship. However, at the same time there are some out there who are not honorable. You can face challenges, and you can be victimized. Therein lies the twisting road. It is going to take some time, so don't make your search a rush job. Do not take every word as gospel.

I talked to a gal a few weeks ago on one of the dating sites, and she met what she believed was a nice honest fellow. Now, had I had known her a few weeks earlier, I would have suggested that she didn't do what she did. On the surface, it sounded romantic, but what she told me was that after talking to a man, somehow he convinced her to fly to California to meet him. I am not sure whether she paid for it herself, but she said a number of times when she got home, she found jewelry missing. The upside is she is still alive to tell the story. You must be careful when you are dealing with anyone on the Internet, and really when dealing with anyone today. I was scammed seven times. Now, I am able to see through the scams. Don't count on luck, and don't take chances.

I suggest that you do a lot of research before you climb on a plane and fly someplace. I met a nice-looking woman from a recommendation, and then I went ahead and called a second gal. She seemed to me the closest to me, about one hundred miles away, and I wasn't sure I wanted to travel that far. The next thing I know, this second woman wanted me to help her obtain her deceased husband's money, and she was willing to marry me, and then we were to get a lawyer, and so forth. In the process of getting together, she sent me two pictures. In one photo she had brown hair, and in another she was a blonde. I had talked to her over the phone, and one time she sounded like an American gal, but the next time like she was from Europe. Now, you be the judge! I backed away from this gal, but she kept calling me. I turned this whole thing over to the police, and that was the last of it!

The Dating Site Photo

I must tell you that I was more than surprised at the number of you women who are not being fair to yourselves regarding your photo. First, this is an opinion of mine, and of course it is going to be based on my experience. At this point, I have looked at about five hundred photos of women on three dating sites, and I have interviewed a few other men. I also have a little bit of experience and have somewhat exposed men too. Plus, I must admit that I believe you will too, for beauty is in the eye of the beholder.

Men are more moved by looks than you women are. This isn't to say that you are also not interested in a nice-looking gentleman. "Hey, Sally, look at those eyes." May I assume I am a little bit right? Okay, think about this: You should want to put your best foot forward. If so, please don't submit a picture that is so dark you can't even tell who it is. Yes, there are a great many of you I couldn't make out in your photos. Submit a picture no farther away than from the waist up. Yes, we want to see what you look like. I am sorry to say this, but I pass by a photo of anyone whom I can't tell if it is male or female, or I could not see the person clearly. It is your call, but I don't think sending in a picture of a nonperson, one of those photo placeholder fillers, is doing you any favors. You pay good money to join one or more sites, and you are sending out nonpictures. Yes, you may want to ask a guy to ask you to share a photo with them, but this is not the first answer that comes to my mind. What comes to me is, "Next." I would say that more than 95 percent of the time, this is true for me. I can't speak for all men here, but I am going to suggest that it is true for a high number. A good many guys tell me that they are not looking to see your flowers, cat, dog, or house. They want to see the person. I can't agree more.

Again, this is my observation, but we are not shopping for cats, dogs, flowers, horses, statues, and so forth. We are looking for the right woman. Sure, an animal enhances the photo of you and maybe tells a little story that you ride, hike, or garden. But I am looking for a nice gal to have on my arm, not a pet. I have two great dogs myself. Most men who are looking at your picture want to see you, not a pet cockatoo!

In your profile, you can talk about riding, your animals, and traveling. And sure, seeing you on that camel suggests to me that you are willing to take some risks and enjoy traveling. This is great, but I want to see what you look like, and most of my fellow brothers do too. So get a professional photographer to take your pictures. A few of you are looking down, up, or away, and you are not smiling or are almost crying.

Some Advice

Let's look at Sally, who wrote the following.

> Hi, it's called "getting the cart before the horse." I have marveled at some of the men who know without a doubt that they want to make love to me while we are talking for the first time. Many of them want me to travel two or three hundred miles to see them. Many cannot text at all. Many are so afraid that they cannot bring themselves

to ask you for coffee, and they are across town from me. I think we all get in a huge hurry instead of letting the chips fall where they may. You are exactly right—what we are trying to do is find someone with whom we feel comfortable, someone who does things the way we do, speaks the way we speak, eats the things we eat, and lives in a house like ours. You really must use your imagination in this game. Does this make sense? Maybe not. Anyway, I have enjoyed much of the time I have spent on her.

Yes, Sally, some of your stuff makes a good deal of sense, but you also need to be a little flexible. First, I am going to say that it is extreme to ask a woman or a man to travel up to three hundred miles to meet anyone. I also think this is a little if not a lot dangerous, and they could be setting you up for some very uncomfortable events. It could be putting your life on the line. Maybe do this after several months of dating, or do it closer to your city or home.

But at the same time, you both don't need to wear the same clothing or eat the same food. With this new acquaintance of mine, she is a vegetation. Yes, I eat meat, but we both like ice cream and popcorn. I suggest that you focus on whether you like being together. Walking hand in hand, a touch, and a smile. Does he respect you, and do you respect him? Do you enjoy looking into his eyes and feeling his touch? I eat crab, she has a salad, and this works well. Sally, maybe set a distance that you would feel comfortable driving. Now, I like to have her over, we sometimes go to my gun club, and of course I take her to dinner and a movie. We are about forty-five minutes apart, maybe an hour. This is about my limit. And you must have some limits. Sure, you can break the rules, but at least you have some place to start from.

And Sally, this is not making love. Making love includes some romance, hence the term *love*, and also honor, tenderness, and respect. These are dogs in heat. Save your love for a man who is willing to share his heart with you.

As my female friends and I got closer, we discussed things. One was food, and I said, If it tastes good, I am going to eat it. Today, I do eat more non meat items, and it is better for me. I understand this is true. But at the same time, as recent as last night, I had a ribeye steak and a glass of wine. I normally drink very little, but now I have a glass of wine with her, sometimes two. And about three nights ago, she prepared an all-vegetable dinner with rice. I enjoyed it and told her so, but a nice piece of meat might have made it better for me.

Here is Cindy.

> A verbose man. How unusual! I would welcome spending time with someone who doesn't (a) try to sell me on his virtues/assets before we ever even meet, (2) doesn't spill his guts on a first date, and (3) understands emotional risk. I like both commonalities and differences, and I like in-person pacing versus jumping off a cliff immediately. Not big on mega up-front emails or phone calls. I prefer eyeball-to-eyeball interaction. From me, you can expect to know exactly what I am thinking.
>
> I laugh a lot; life is too short not to do so. More likely than not, I roll with the punches. I am fearless, without throwing all caution to the wind. If I were not up for a challenge, I wouldn't be doing this. And I often laugh at myself; I am human and make mistakes too.

Hi, Cindy. I have decided to take a little approach with this book, so when I am talking to you, I hope to be talking to the other women who are reading this. Yes, I am hoping that I can get a little help from some women. I am sure that I can't help you all, and some will not try to change or take any advice. I am sure that this is the same with some men.

First, stick to your guns. I am assuming you are on one or more sites for the same reason that a lot of us are. I lost my second wife to two cancers and a four-year battle. Now, as you may have discovered, I am an educator with over eighteen years in various levels of education and teaching, plus more than fifty years of marriage, so I am hoping my experience and training will help. I am going to talk to you as I would an average man. I am not interested in a debate over this. Here we go.

I can assure you I have made a number of mistakes along the way. In fact, I am going to say that more than likely, I more often learned from making mistakes rather than getting it right the first time.

I think that we have gotten caught in the fast track, the thirty-second commercial, with a great deal of artificial and plastic America. We have had a good number of folks involved in deceit and deception, and with the ability to hide behind the computer, they can pump untruth and create a degree of phoniness.

That makes it difficult for the honest folks to become skeptical of everything they see in text. This has made it very difficult to separate the wheat from the shaft and the bull from the "non-bull". I am sure you get my drift. There are so many commercials during a program now, sometimes I feel like we should be watching the commercials and not the material in the program. And these so-called commercials the product in each situation is always the best.

Back in the good old days, a gentleman would somehow come across a young lady he found attractive, and he would ask if he could come visit her at her home, or maybe meet at the soda fountain. Maybe he would call her, or he would come over to her home and swing on the swing on the porch after meeting her father and mother. I can remember taking a diesel bus and a Talley bus that ran on electricity across town just to meet and talk to a gal. I would talk to her on the porch and ask her to go to a picture show. That way, you had an idea whom you were talking to and seeing. You would share your story while sitting eye to eye, not on a cell phone.

Yes, now it is different. Some stories are filled with half-truths. The young man or woman may be some distance away, and the stories may not be true. What you read on the computer screen, hear on the phone, or read in a letter may be false. That leaves you with a dilemma: What can you believe?

My advice to you is to first know what you are looking for and your goal. Are you looking for a companion, friend, or pen pal, and what does this entail? Will there be some casual dating, or are you serious about a relationship? Each person has different requirements. First make your decision with your mind. Sure, the heart is going to play a role here, but real love takes some time to grow.

The best thing I can suggest is if you feel good about the person you are talking to, it is still a risk. Remember this. Is this some kind of role-playing on their part? Come up with a safe and mutual location. Today, having someone meet you at your home is becoming unsafe, so you may not want to go there yet. Also, it can be a good idea to have a friend or relative go with you on the first or even second meeting if it goes that far.

Now, I don't believe you can get a real judge of the kind of person you have met until you have spent some time with the person. People can put their best foot forward if they try. You may talk and share stories, jokes, ideas, and information. You may observe their movements and body language, and this can give you some good information. How did you feel about eye contact? Were you the center of his intention? If not, this may tell you more than what he is saying. Was he shifting around in his chair? This can be a good sign that it isn't you he is interested in.

One of the downsides we face is that we don't have the time we had when we were kids, but at the same time, we don't want to sell ourselves short. I don't know about you, but I would like this relationship to be my last. You have to believe that. If you have been in a relationship—at least in my case—start off getting together. Here are these two entities from different worlds trying to merge two lives, habits, and ideas. They are trying to become one mind. Now, my new wife—oh, yes, I didn't tell you until now that I married the gal I met during my research about three months ago. Anyway, my new wife gets kind of mad at me for putting things in the sink and not the dishwasher during the day. At the end of the day or the next day, I put them in the dishwasher, or if I need something washed, I might do it then, but she likes the sink empty. So we have a different mind-set, and this doesn't trouble me, but it does her. Now I have to change my habit. I don't mind because if it makes her happy, I benefit too! And I don't mind sharing what I have, but I do not want to lose it and end up in poverty or worse. "Am I really the one the person is looking for or is it my wallet?" This can be a real question, and you may not like the answer, but it is better to learn now than later!

How long should this first meeting or date last? Well, there are no rules here, but if it isn't going well, give yourself an hour, have a drink or a meal, and thank the person for the time. You can say that you enjoyed the meal and the meeting and that you will contact them. Give your phone number, e-mail address, or whatever you feel comfortable with—or continue the experience. It is in your hands.

This comes from Carol.

> Hi, Gene. I am new to online dating and not too comfortable. I have been a widow for four years. Husband of fifty-two years died of cancer. Looking to see if someone has similar interests to fill the lonely times. I enjoy a good time with friends, traveling, dining, playing cards or games, and cruising. What about you?

Well, here we are. I have a similar situation. I lost my wife very quickly from two cancers. I was married to her for a little over twenty-three years, and I am looking for a long-term relationship, as well as what this gal came up with, but this is just the open conversation.

You cannot take anything for granted on the Internet, and I am sorry to say this is too bad, but it is what it is! In the short time that I have been here, I have experienced seven attempted scams. Yes, this is disappointing, but at the same time these sites provide good, honest people an avenue to find a new love, companion, partner, friend, and more. You must watch for the signs and make decisions with caution. There is an old saying that seems true: "If it sounds too good to be true, it more than likely is not true." And another one is very simple: "Trust your gut."

You may find stories have the same kind of ring to them. For example, I met on the computer and on my cell phone a young lady with nice looks. But later, there was a kind of mistake on her part, with two different women playing the same part. She was well to do, had lost her husband, and needed someone to marry so she could stay here and get control of these funds. Now, you don't get all this information up front, just bits and pieces. First we kind of hit it off, and very soon she was coming to visit. Maybe she is short on cash and asks, "Send me a PIN number, and I can get this or that. I love you. Don't you love me? You don't trust me? We can get married and live happily ever after." Eventually it comes to things like, "I need five hundred dollars to renew my passport." It will always be something. "I am out of the country right now." Now, in this case it is a woman, but it could easily be a guy, or anyone.

I have a woman friend who met this fellow on a site, and after some talking back and forth, somehow he convinced her to fly several thousand miles to meet him. I am assuming they got somewhat serious, and when she got home, her earring and some personal items were gone. This is almost like a TV show, where the pictures are up on the wall mapping her whole life. How close was she to being found in a freezer?

Out of state and in unfamiliar territory—not a good plan. It was a big risk. But you have to make that decision and have a plan.

Here is Bobbi's message.

Thank you for your email. Best wishes for success in your search. Hey, if you met someone … go for it. No need to tell me how to date. I have been a grown single person for fourteen years.

Bobbi, when you find a gentleman who is seemingly interested in you but wants to be honest with you by sharing the fact that he met another person on the site, don't fret. It is to kind of test the water, and he didn't say that they were committed in any way, engaged, or getting married. He was saying, "Hey, you are interested in me, and I kind of want to meet you, but this situation happened before I met you. I am not completely sure if we are a match but would like to see if you and I have something that might be closer to what I am looking for. I am willing to meet you if you are interested, but so you know, this other thing is going on." Please give this some thought. This fellow is interested in you, and he is willing to be completely honest about what is going on in his life. Understand that he could have concealed the fact he has met someone else and maybe dated another person before he found you on the site. He is not engaged or married, and he is not trying not to conceal the fact that he is meeting other people. That should say a lot of positive things about him. Isn't this what the site is all about—trying to meet the right person and maybe develop a relationship?

You can't have a relationship without meeting people, and as the saying goes, "You may have to kiss a lot of frogs in the process." I am not saying this gentleman is a frog, but this is up to you to find that out. You can't meet anyone if your door is closed.

It sounds like you are disciplining him for being honest and truthful. He wasn't telling you how to date or run your life. You may have to open your heart and mind a bit to let this person in. This is your choice.

Sandy sent this message.

> Hello, thanks for your reply. I am so sorry about your cancer. My brother-in-law went through this same treatment and has no cancer now, so don't give up hope. Keep in touch with me, and we may plan to meet later, after you feel strong. Have you started your treatment yet? How are you feeling? If you feel like a trip to east Texas or somewhere in between, let me know, and we can meet for lunch or dinner.
>
> Over two hours is not a problem for me to come to the Dallas area. My daughter lives in the Colony near Lewisville or North Dallas. Have a good week.
>
> Let me know your thoughts. You can reach me on cell.

Sandy, thank you. It is nice to hear from you, I have to say that it is nice to hear from a lady who is willing to meet a gentleman and is willing to go out of her way to drive so far. Yes, I do understand that you have a daughter in the area, which does make it somewhat easier.

As you know, I have been dating someone, but this is not formal or exclusive. There are one or two deal breakers that are on the table, so I am not trying to pull anything off here, but we can have a nice meeting and experience and work from there. As I said, one of the issues that I have had with several gals is that we have been very far apart, and I have opted not to try to date anyone more than about fifty miles away.

But because you seemed so excited and nice, and also willing to meet and enjoy a nice evening or lunch with conversation, I am delighted to meet with you.

I have to say that I very much believe in meeting with people in this case, because it is hard for me to get an idea of what people are really like online. Sure, you can get some information from the site, but it doesn't start coming together until the two of you get a chance to meet and talk across a table.

Because you are open and friendly, I will give you a call, and I look forward to our meeting in a couple of weeks. (I must be honest here, for some reason, this meeting didn't happen.)

Now, let's meet Jane:

> I think you may have confused me with someone else
> because I don't not have your email or phone number. Yes,
> I still teach, but only part-time Mondays and Wednesdays.

I have to say it was nice that you were willing to correspond, trying to clear up some kind of a miscommunication and take the time to add some information about yourself and career. That shows a degree of interest, and because we have related careers, this brings up commonality between the two of us and may suggest some interest.

What you have done—and you may have wanted to—is open the door to allow this gentleman to respond. I am going to assume this was what you wanted to do. Good show.

Here is Peggy's message:

> Yes, I am on the edge of Grapevine and Euless. [For those who are not acquainted with the Texas area, these cities are in the Dallas area.] I would love to visit with you next week. I get back Sunday and can have an afternoon with you. Well, here comes my group, so we will talk later!

Peggy, hi. I just received your note today. I misunderstood your first note. I see now that you are available and are not now involved with any one person. May I ask, are you divorced?

She replied,

> I am a one-man woman, once I determine that we are compatible, and I would look forward to building a relationship. Of course, initially we need to meet, see what the other is like, and share some experiences before we can make that decision. I would love to hear more about you. I see you have a doctorate. What did you teach? How many children do you have? I have a son and daughter and eight grandchildren. I have a lot of fun in life and very much appreciate a man who has a good sense of humor. Does it bother you that you live in Fort Worth and I live around the Woodlands? I feel it is doable, and I think it could work out if the interest is there. I would love to hear more from you. Have a wonderful day!

I must give you three stars for being willing to share and being open enough to admit that I could have misread what you sent. And a couple of stars for the willingness to discuss further to get more facts to evaluate. Now, it seems that many gals are not really on the same page here. Tell me, I am here on the dating site to find a gal to date, companion, or even more.

I am going to suggest that most gentlemen are here to find a relationship, something long-term, whereas others are dating short-term. Some want just a physical relationship, and maybe a few are up to no good. But I have to say that based on my work here, I have found that many women are not sure why they are here. They might stick their toe into the water, but at the same time they are not willing to get it wet. So far, I don't see you in this category.

I have discovered that a good many women will suggest they are loving and are looking for a nice guy or companion to share time, maybe travel, go dancing, go out to dinner, and such. But when the rubber really meets the road, the children need a babysitter, they have to go on a cruise with a group of their girlfriends, or they have to take care of their summer house in Florida. Yes, I would love to meet someone, but I really don't have an hour to meet at a nice place and talk when you really get down to it.

But you seem open to exploring a meeting with the opposite sex in a noncommittal way and a nonhostile environment. Thank you.

The following is from Grace.

> Thank you for your message. I am very new at this and totally unsure about meeting anyone. At this point, I am curious but am not thinking of any serious relationship. I appreciate your message, but I am not interested at this time.

This message is not to Grace but to you, the reader. Before you take up time—your time, and the time of the gentleman who might be interested in breaking the ice and communicating with you—decide what you want and where you want to go with a relationship. Why waste your time and the time of other people if you are not sure or not serious about some kind of a relationship? No, you don't have to jump right in, but no one is going to be hurt if you just want to talk, have a drink, or have dinner with a member of the opposite sex. Try to be clear about your intention.

I met a gal for a nice afternoon dinner, and after spending over an hour together, she announced she really didn't have the time to pursue a relationship with anyone.

Grace, here is what I would suggest. There is nothing wrong with being a little apprehensive with this dating site business. But don't penalize yourself too much for being somewhat normal. I have had seven different women try to scam me, and I gave an example here of a gal who found things missing when she got home from her date. But remember the first day of school? You didn't want to go to class and be exposed to any of those new students. Or how about when you had a hard time jumping in the pool the first time? I am sure you ran right up and got in? No, more than likely, your mother or father had to nearly force you to put a toe in, then your foot, and so on until you were all wet. Well, it is the same thing here. Put your toe in first, and if it feels good, take the next step. Then you will soon be jumping in from the high board. But you owe it to yourself to take the first step. Do it at your own speed, not the speed of your girlfriends or neighbors. When you go on the site, present yourself with your own terms and some information. First talk to a few guys. There is nothing to it. Maybe you are not sure if you are interested in a serious relationship, but you can talk and meet, and perhaps you can have lunch or dinner in a nice, quiet place. Perhaps you will find some common ground and then to go a movie if the first meeting goes well, or you can simply be social friends. There have been times in the last two years I have welcomed just the company and conversation, as opposed to sitting by myself with my dogs watching a movie on TV.

Here is Helen's message:

> Other than the distance between us, I think we match up well. I am a little confused about where you are located. Saginaw, Missouri is close to Joplin, Missouri. Is that where you live?
>
> I live in Springfield, Missouri, now but lived close to Redding's Mill for several years. Is this close to the

> Saginaw shown on your profile? Hey, if we are that close to one another, we could meet in Mt. Vernon for the heck of it and discussed this online dating situation.

No, folks, Saginaw, Texas, is a small city inside Fort Worth, so it would be several hundred miles from Springfield, Missouri. I must say, I talked and met through some photos some very nice gals, and in most cases most of them would have been nice to meet for dinner if they were closer. I explained it to her, and she followed up with several more messages.

> That's okay, and I've never done something like this before. I appreciate you choosing my profile. Best wishes. I hope all goes well with you. I will be traveling to see my oldest daughter in Austin and my oldest son in Houston during the week.

> Hi, I have returned from Cancun safe and sound. Meeting was good and hopefully will help my client whom I went for. Wedding went off perfectly for my friend's daughter. She was a beautiful bride, and I am glad that is behind me now. How is your week going? Does it look like you will have time in your schedule this week for us to meet? You mentioned association. I remember going with my ex-husband and spending many a day at skeet ranges and competitions. I was so pregnant with our son at one competition, other wives were offering to take me away from the noise! I enjoyed it, though, so guns are no problem for me. I shot a bird with a .410 once.

> Hope all is well with you. I wish you a Happy Thanksgiving! I will be traveling to see my oldest daughter in Austin and my oldest son in Houston during the week.

Listen, I must be fair with you and everyone I meet. It is nice to have someone interested in you, but I have to tell the truth. About three months ago, at that time and even now, I am not totally sure of the outcome or where this might go, but I met a gal on one of the sites. I must be fair with you and everyone I come in contact with. It is nice to have someone interested in me, but at that time I committed that I would not try to meet or date another while we run this relationship up the flagpole, and we are working on it. At this point I committed that I would not try to meet others, and I am not a playboy because l am looking for a real relationship. So to be honest and fair, I must tell you this. Also, the distance may be a problem. This gal is about fifty miles away, and this can sometimes be an issue. In fact, we have talked about moving in together for a few days a week to see if we are compatible. We may sell both places that we have and buy another that we both agree on and that fits our lifestyle together.

I have to admit that there is a certain amount of risk at our age, as well as when we were younger. I am not sure if there are any statistics as to who can have a better relationship, under forty-five or over forty-five, but I would have to believe we older people should have a better handle on what we are looking for or not looking for, because we have had some experience. We have decided what we like and dislike, and we have been there and done that. I hope that we have time to learn something from our past.

My Prince Charming

I hope this is true and that you get your wish sooner than later, but you must be realistic when we are setting parameters for our Prince Charming. For example, a good many women were very much overwhelmed by the tall, dark, and handsome John Wayne. He was over six feet tall and was rough and tough. But you may find that Roy Rogers is your man; he was a good horseman, and he could sing and play a guitar, but he wasn't over six feet tall. He too was in films. Or there was Audie Murphy, the most decorated soldier in World War II. Because of his outstanding service, he became a movie star, but he was short in stature. And there was Frank Sinatra; back in the day, women went wild over his singing.

Now, I always liked tall blondes, but not too tall. My first wife was a brunette and was five foot seven. My blonde second wife was five foot six. I myself am six foot three and have a Middle Eastern tan, if you will. So yes, opposites attract, as they say. But as soon as you say this, two people who claim to have the same likes and dislikes will appear. Beauty truly is in the eye of the beholder. I believe my mother had a Prince Charming, but she married my dad, and he was a far cry from being the six-foot knight on a white horse, but there was something—there had to be. I have no idea because she never told me.

Put together some of the things you are looking for in a man. Yes, make a list and write it down. Is he tall, funny, serious, and good-looking? What color is his hair? Is he rich and smart? Does he come from a large family? This can be important to some. What is his social level and education? When I met my first wife, she was college educated, and at the time I had a high school diploma but a desire to get a college education. If you find a guy who meets all your criteria but is bald or short, or who drinks, is this a deal breaker? I am going to talk about deal breakers later in the book. For now, I suggest that you have deal makers and deal breakers in every category. Of course, you are in control, and you have this standard to go by, but it is your choice whether or not you follow it to the letter. Remember, this is your life and your future we are talking about.

A Prince Charming sounds nice, but at the same time, are we going to meet their standard? This situation is going to cut both ways. For example, what if Prince Charming is so busy that he can spend only a day with you on a weekend, and he has to play karaoke with the boys once a week, shoot pool and have a beer night with his brother on Fridays, and golf on Saturday? Is this a deal breaker? And this is before you get very serious. This is one of the things I see a lot with you gals, so think about it a lot. Sure, you get to wear a crown, sit in a nice velvet chair, be waited on by servants, and live in a castle. But what are you looking for? A companion to fill in between your cruises? Is this going to work for you, and furthermore, is it going to work for Mr. Right? It cuts both ways, because as they say, what is good for the goose is good for the gander.

Let's look at a few things. Some men are into fishing and hunting, and others are into sports. I was over at my son-in-law's place recently, and there were five or six guys screaming as their favorite team was running to make a touchdown. I did play football and basketball, and I was kind of into the game. My son played college ball for Mexico State. However, I would prefer a nice steak in a quiet restaurant, followed by a movie. I recommend you think about this. Are you into being at one of these activities where everyone is jumping up and down and screaming? I know some women like to do these things, but if you don't, remember that this can be nearly every weekend.

"Would you bait my hook?" I have heard some of you gals say this. Well let me tell you that I wouldn't. I don't fish, so this is not a selling point for me to have you alongside me. But I would be more disappointed if one of the reasons that am dating you is because of your suggestion of being interested in going to the gun range to shoot, but when the rubber meets the road, you really don't like guns. If you do like guns, outstanding. If not, you have wasted both our time. I like to go to the range, as well as hunt wild pigs. It is better to say you don't know how to change a tire and have no idea what a pressure gauge is.

Here is another example of how this works. I just got married to a woman I met in my online search for my special person, and one of the things I was very happy with was the fact that we both like to go to the gun range. For our engagement, I gave her a S&W 380 Easy Pull automatic. This is what she takes to the range when we go together. And this is one reason I married her. It was not the only one, but it is a deal maker.

It is also important that you really know what your parameters are. Are you interested in dating, a serious relationship, or a companion? And what is the difference between a companion, friend, date, and serious relationship to you? Are you really into a serious relationship? I believe that most gentlemen would like to know where they are going, and any reasonable gentleman would be willing to share his position. Each of these choices has serious considerations. Before I met my current wife, I was developing a relationship with another gal who also lives in the Dallas area. We seemed to get along very well, but when I kind of pressed her and suggested I wanted to take the relationship to a higher level, she didn't. I felt kind of bad, but it was better that we both found where we both were before we wasted a lot of time. It is important that you talk.

If it is a serious consideration, how long is a reasonable period of time to date before a sexual relationship should happen? The answer to this question is very simple but varies with the individual. This must be worked out between the two people. There is no hard and fast rule. I ran into this one just the other day. I know this couple, and one lives in Dallas and is very close to her daughter. The gentleman lives in Fort Worth, and he is very close to his daughter-in-law and the kids. This question comes up: "If we get together, where would you like to live?" the female suggests, and rightly so, near her daughter. He says, "I really don't care," but his son-in-law and daughter-in-law who help him with various things like going to the doctor or working on his house want him close because of the time it takes to help him; they have their own responsibilities too. So what do they do with the second house and, more seriously, the benefits, social security, health insurance, and other financial areas? This comes after you find your real prince. You are going to seek a lawyer and maybe develop a trust, but now you have family, property, and money involved. So you are again facing decisions that are important to both your futures. Maybe tall, dark, and handsome is not the right prince after all. It might be that nice, quiet guy sitting across the room. You may need to spread your wings a bit when making these decisions.

Let's look at Margie, who wrote this:

> Hi, sounds like you have already met someone, so good luck with your relationship. I am not sure if I am ready for a relationship. I am new here.

This is what we have been talking about. This lady really doesn't know what she wants to do. Oh, yes, this can be a hard decision for many of us, but it also can be confusing for the people you are trying to meet or talk to. If need be, talk to some friends whom you respect or who have gone through the same question. You can also seek a counselor or a minister.

First, thank you for your input, Margie, but it is my opinion that before you get involved in a dating site, you should do a lot of soul searching to make sure this is something you really want to do. This is not an easy step for anyone, and of course you must be careful and not let down your guard. I am going to suggest that many if not most people on these sites are honestly looking for some kind of relationship, and when a gentleman sees a woman, it isn't easy for him to go out on a limb. Now he has been shot down before he has even had a chance to express himself. This can make his next attempt even more difficult. You need to consider your interests before you open the door and then close it before the individual on the other end has a chance to express himself.

As far as I am concerned, if I really have an up-and-going relationship, I wouldn't be trying to open the door to another person. At this time, with the person I am dating, she and I are not committed, and there are a couple of deal breakers on the table, so I am not totally sure I have a real relationship here.

Sheri wrote the following.

In a relationship I am looking for:

I would expect honest love, faithfulness, and the truth. I would like to have a person who believes in me, as well as one whom I can believe in. In this case, full support. To be honest with me at all times, and I would do the same.

What you are asking is very reasonable, and by putting this out there, you are asking up front any gentlemen interested to be willing to be on the same page with you. Asking for and expecting honesty and full support is more than reasonable. Good luck with your search.

Questions You May Want to Ask While Determining Whether You Want to Meet a Dating Candidate

In this dating game, the decisions you make over the next few months or so can affect the balance of your adult life and that of the person with whom you are involved. I have to put together important questions you can ask. Get answers from the other person, but also ask them to yourself. Determine whether the two answers are going to be acceptable for you. Are your answers, or the combination of answers, going to work for your new partner as well as you? Do not take this lightly. I believe a number of people on these sites have not spent time evaluating the consequences of going on the sites and getting involved with people before they really know and understand what has driven them to participate in the Dating Game.

To the individual taking this survey, if any of the following questions are offensive to you, you have the right to avoid answering them.

1. What is your date of birth and age? _____
    _____ –
2. What is your ethnic background? _____
3. Your weight? _____
4. Your height? _____
5. Do you attend church regularly? _____
6. Do you use drugs? _____
7. How important is being a member of your church? _____
8. How do you feel about dating a nonmember of your faith?
    _____
9. How many times have you been married? _____
10. Why are you trying to date? _____
11. How many children do you now have alive? _____
12. Are you still married? _____

13. If you found a person and you cared for him or her, would you entertain marriage or being together long-term if the other person didn't become a member of your faith?

14. Do you take care of any of your grandchildren now? _____ How many? _____

15. Do you work outside the home? ____

16. Do you have any dependents? _____

17. How many hours a week do you work outside the home? _____

18. Do you have any activities or hobbies with the same sex or friends? _____

19. Would you give any activities up if you met the right person? _____

20. Do you use a walker or wheelchair to get around? _____

21. Do you need oxygen to get about? _____

22. Can you drive a vehicle? _____

23. Do you live with your parents? _____

24. Do you own a home or rent? _____

25. What do you think when someone states that he or she is looking for a companion? _____

26. Would you be interested in remarrying? Why or why not?

    _____

    _____

27. Do you have any real health issues?

28. Add your own question? _____

29. _____

30. _____

31. _____

32. _____

33. Do you enjoy animals? _____

34. Do you have any animals? _____ _____ _____

    _____

35. Do you like cats? _____

36. Can you ride a horse? _____

37. Do you enjoy ranching or farming? _____

38. Would you be willing to raise an alpaca? _____

39. Would you date a person who had to use a cane or walker? _____

40. Do you fly, or can you operate an aircraft? _____

41. Do you like to go in a glider? _____

42. Do you like fishing? _____
43. How do you feel about baiting a fishing hook? _____
44. Do you enjoy football, basketball, or baseball? _____
45. What is one of your favorite teams? _____ A favorite player? _____
46. Would you watch a pornography movie? _____
47. What is your favorite type of film? _____ _ _____
48. Favorite food? _____
49. Do you hunt? Are you willing to go out and shoot a wild animal? _____
50. Do you do drugs? _____
51. Do you smoke? _____
52. Do you roll your own? _____
53. Is education important to you? _____
54. Do you drink alcohol? _____
55. What was your major in high school? _____
56. Major in College? _____ _____
57. Did you finish high school? _____
58. Did you get your GED? _____
59. How many brothers or sisters do you have alive? _____
60. Are you close to your family? _____
61. Is family important to you? _____
62. Are your parents alive? _____
63. Do you play chess? _____ Cards? _____ Poker? _____
64. Do you smoke? _____ Do you chew? _____
65. Do you like to work in the yard? _____ Why or why not? _____
66. Can you cook? _____ Name one of your favorite foods? _____ Desserts? _____
67. In a marriage, who should take care of all the funds? _____
68. If you were going to buy a vehicle right now, what kind or type would you buy? _____ Why?
69. When you take off your dress shirt or blouse, what is the next step you prefer? _____
70. Dress pants or everyday pants? Would you have just the dress pants dry-cleaned, or the everyday pants cleaned and pressed too? _____

71. We have a date this afternoon. You showered in the morning. Would you shower more than once? Why? _____

72. If you had a lot of gray hair, would you color your hair to look a little younger? _____

73. Do you ever bring flowers to a date's home? _____

74. How should we pay on the first date? Split the bill, or the man or the woman pays? _____

75. Do you drink wine? _____ About how many glasses a week? _____

76. Are you a Democrat? _____ Liberal? _____ Conservative? _____

77. In American folklore, who was John Henry? _____ Did he win? _____

78. If I come into your home, should I take off my shoes? _____

79. Do you like fried chicken? _____

80. Do you swim? _____

81. Do you shoot or carry a handgun _____?

82. Do you care if I do? _____

83. Would you date someone who carries a firearm? _____

84. Should males and females be treated the same? _____

85. Should women have the right to be in the military? _____ In all positions? _____

86. Should there be separate bathrooms in public places, or one for both sexes? _____

87. Should we allow same-sex marriage? _____ Do you care? _____

88. Is it okay to have sex before marriage? _____

89. Is it okay to have sex on the first date? _____ Why or why not? _____

90. Would you like to marry again? _____ Why or why not? _ _____

91. What might stop you from marrying again? _____

92. Would you live with a person if you couldn't get married?

93. Name one thing that would stop you from getting married but not from living together. _____

94. If a potential partner tells you she or he loves you but wants to use her or his own name, is this a deal breaker for getting together? _____

95. If asked to join a partner's religion, would this be a deal breaker? _____

96. Name two deal breakers. _____
_____

97. Which ones of the following could be deal breakers?
Honesty _____ Fidelity ____ Family _____ Drugs _____ State _____ Income _____ Health _____ Music _____ Sex _____ Looks _____ Personality _____ Cleanliness _____ Smoking _____ Weight _____ Politics _____ Having sex more than twice a week _____ Wearing the opposite sex's clothing _____ Doing drugs _____ Adultery____ _____ Add your own _____

98. Do you have a hobby? _____ Would you give up some things to have more time to be with your significant other? _____

99. How much time would be the right amount to spend with your significant other? _____ If he or she wants more, are you willing to negotiate? _____

100. State two things that you would not negotiate with a significant other.
_____ _____

101. If you went out to look at beds together, what would be too much to pay for one? _____

102. What would be a fair price to pay for a home today? _____

103. Do you watch professional sports on TV? _____

104. Do you enjoy law movies or programs, like *Law and Order*? _____

105. What kinds of movies do you like? _____

106. Name two types of movies you don't care for. _____
_____

107. Do you like to travel? _____

108. Do you gamble? _____

109. Do you dance? _____

110. Do you hunt? _____

111. Do you like fairs, museums, comedy clubs, plays, gun shows? Circle anyone you don't like, or add your own. _____

112. What is your favorite color?
113. Is there any place you would not like to be touched by your significant other? _____
114. Do you like to be romantic? _____
115. Hold hands? _____
116. Kiss? _____
117. Would you enjoy having your significant other wash your back in the shower? _____
118. Do you dance? _____
119. Ride horses? _____
120. Camp? _____
121. Bowl? _____
122. Go to church? _____
123. Babysit more than once a week for one of your children? _____
124. How much time do you spend with your family? _____
125. Can you cook? _____
126. Do you eat meat?_____
127. In a sexual relationship, is there anything you prefer not being involved in? _____
128. Is it okay for your mate to have a male or female sexual relationship? Do you want an open marriage? _____
129. Do you snore? _____
130. Is there anything that is off-limits if you were with your significant other? _____
131. What would make you happy that your significant other could do right now, to make you happy and feel better about the relationship? _____
132. Your significant other would like to go on a road trip about 1,500 miles away. How do you feel about that? _____
133. She or he would like to buy a nice twenty-six-foot camper trailer and use it for long and short trips. What would be your position?

    _____ _____
    _____ _____
    _____

134. She or he would like to live near her or his children, and you might have to move. What would be your position?

_____

_____

135. Would you like to purchase a new vehicle?

_____

_____

136. Is it okay for you or your spouse to have a separate (or secret) bank account? _____

137. How many dogs are okay to have in your home? _____

138. How many cats? _____

139. How many birds? _____

140. Do you want a new home

_____

_____

141. Should you buy new future together?

_____

_____

142. Have you had cosmetic surgery?

_____

_____

143. Have you loaned money to a friend or relative?

_____

_____

144. Have you bet five hundred dollars or more on a sure winner in a horse race on a tip?

_____

_____

145. Are you a perfectionist? Do you want everything in place? Do you want the recycling in the right container, not with the garbage?

_____

146. Do you want to put a new fence up in the backyard?

_____

_____

147. Would you let a friend or relative move in?

_____

148. Your partner wants to buy a new firearm because the one he or she has shoots expensive ammo that is getting hard to find? This is his or her only hobby. Do you allow the purchase?

_____

149. Which is the most important room in the house?_____
    Why? _____

150. Is it okay to put the dishes in the sink until the end of the day? Or do you want to put dirty dishes in the washer throughout the day? _____

151. What pets are allowed in your home? _____

152. Which type of home would you not want to live in? _____

153. Who has the final word in the relationship?_____

154. The best way to run a home is to compromise. True or false? _____

155. In a relationship, which is better: to compromise, or to have one leader? _____

156. Are tattoos okay? Do they have to be covered up? _____

157. There should not be a firearm in the home. True or false? ____

158. Is it okay to loan money to a relative or friend without first talking to your partner? _____

159. Are women better at managing money? _____

160. The man's job is more important than the woman. True or false? _____

161. Should all lights be off in the bedroom at night? _____

162. Name one good reason to live with your parents. _____

163. Should couples take time to talk to each other at the dinner table? _____

164. Should there be reading or watching TV at the dinner table? _____

165. Is the woman's place in the home? _____

166. A man should not strike a woman, at any time, but a female can because she is smaller. True or false? _____

167. Is sex not important if you are over fifty years old? _____

168. There is only one way to engage in sex after marriage. True or false? _____

169. Sex is important all the time. True or false? _____

170. Should a sexual relationship be up to both parties? _____

171. Do you like to hold hands and kiss anytime during the day? _____

172. Once you are living together or married, is it important to take care of your looks? _____

173. Do you have a responsibility to manage your appearance for your spouse and yourself? _____

174. Where would you prefer to live?

_____

175. How important is sex to you? _____

176. What is a reasonable amount of time to engage in relations with each other? _____

177. Name three places that you might want to go to.

_____   _____   _____

178. Should you feed the dogs from the table? _____

179. I try to go to the gun range as often as I can. How does this make you feel? _____

Some of these questions could be deal breakers for you. Compare your answers to your partner's, and determine your percentage of agreement and whether that rate is too low or is within your range of acceptance. It is up to you to set your own standard. You will get a better view of compatibility if you use a greater number of questions. I would like a score higher than 80 percent. This means you need to look closely at the questions and how they might affect you. For example, if you use hair color and height as criteria, the overall meaning to your relationship would have little to no impact. But if the questions you pick are related to fidelity, gaming, and drugs, they could be very critical to your relationship and overall compatibility.

Using the Internet and the Computer to Develop a Relationship

Facebook, e-mailing, and texting are methods that can be subject to duplicity and deceit. Face-to-face meetings are perhaps highly viable, but they take much more time and are generally much less convenient.

If she or he is not looking at you when you are across the table, this is something you should be aware of. Eye contact can indicate interest in you—or the lack thereof. I suggest that you be a little suspicious here, and maybe a lot. If they are shuffling their feet, this is another indication of a lack of interest in you. And of course, if they are looking away at someone else across the room, you can pretty much assume that their interest doesn't lie with you. If this is your first meeting, you should have 100 percent of their attention. And of course, they should have yours too. The theory is it is you whom they are interested in, not a person across the room or at the next table.

That would not typically have a happy face to present to you. As has been noted, better a bird in the hand than two in the bush. Not that it hasn't happened. Now, most if not all the sites suggest that they are different and provide information you can home in on to select that "true love." As I said, I haven't been on them all, but the four or so that I have used fail to really evaluate and suggest the right individual for the right person, and the score system means little. You are kind of on your own here. Unless I am proven otherwise, the women, as well as the gentlemen, are more or less thrown together by kind of the age range, and very little is really thought about geographically. I have seen suggested gals from New York, California, and the South Pacific even though I have suggested I have a dating radius of less than sixty miles. I have plugged this number in numerous times. This goes for age also. I have suggested an age range of, say sixty-five to seventy-seven, but I have seen young ladies younger than my daughter, who is fifty-six. Now, it is better than nothing, so in my opinion, it is better to work with it and try more than one site. This isn't to say that you give up on other avenues such as clubs, churches, and friends.

It has been disappointing this time, but I do have to agree it is better than nothing. I am not one to join a bird watching society, a bridge club, or a pickleball team. I don't hang at bars. Some of my friend (I don't have many) have suggested that I try to find someone at Walmart or Albertsons, or at my gun club. Well, I did meet a gal at Walmart, we started talking. I asked her out, and she said okay. Then we got around to the fact that she did have a husband, and somehow the fact that he was into guns, but she said he wasn't a very good shot. Now, I am NRA, but I am not looking for a gun fight at the OK Corral with some gal's husband. I don't want to be shot in the back when I am crossing the street.

I suggested a few paragraphs ago an age range of the women I am looking for. My first wife was about three years older than me, and I was perhaps three years older than my second wife. I was really not thinking about a third wife, but when we moved here to Texas, it was to be close to my wife's oldest daughter and family. When I lost her to cancer, it was hard for me. As I started looking for a companion or serious relationship, I didn't think much about age, but I wasn't looking for a young woman. I wanted a mature woman, and I like women who have blonde hair, are tall, do not talk much, somewhat smart, and street savvy. My new wife is seventy-nine years young, and of course I am eighty now; when I started this book, I was seventy-nine. We are close in age and seem to make a good pair. I suggest you do some good planning, but you may want to stay flexible.

Just What Are Guys Looking For?

Men have been asking themselves for years, "Just what am I looking for in a woman?" This is truly a fair question. Is it looks, brains, tall, short, nice hair, legs, hair color, horny, or what? In closed circles many guys will talk and joke about certain attributes: large breasts, a nice derriere, long and silky hair, and so forth. But there is one thing I am going to say: I personally don't want to look up and see her on the television with all her good parts in view for everyone to see. And I am sure most men will agree. I am sure you would not want to see my stuff all over national and international TV either!

For years there has been talk about finding the right person whom we can face life's challenges with, the good, the bad, and the ugly.

Most men find that making a commitment is one of the most difficult and important decisions that they face in their lives.

For years, women by and large have been sharing what they want in men, and they think all we want is some hot beauty with nice hair and breasts, blonde and blue eyes, and the perfect trophy wife. But this seems to be not true. Look around! There is just too much in life going on in life, and what is important to your future isn't that simple. We need to look at various things and characteristics that are time tested.

So What Do We Men Want in a Woman?

- **Character**
  Being knock-down good looking has nothing to do with this. You can meet beautiful gals, but you can find that they have little to no personality. This can be true in nearly every situation. So I am going to look for a woman with a nice and comforting personality first. Which comes first, the chicken or the egg? In this case, it is

the egg, the great personality—and here again, the personality is in the eye of the beholder).

- Affection

  Sure, sex is very important for most men, but a good number of men want to experience affection. Be it holding hands in public, leaving a love message on this computer or voicemail, or just giving him a massage, show that you care about him through these actions of fondness; they will go far in touching his heart.

  Most of the time, I call my wife and tell her when I am leaving for the doctor's office, and when I leave the office, so we know where each of us is in case of an emergency. We hold hands while watching TV and at night when we go to bed. She kisses me good morning when she goes to work. She is still working and I am retired, but I am around the house, and of course I am writing my books, taking my dogs to the groomer, and so forth. At night, we often play a little game as I kiss her good night, pull up her blanket, and turn off her lights.

  You can try different ways to demonstrate how much you care by being warm. Do simple things like tell him that you love him, give him support when he is feeling doubtful, and tell him that you are sorry when things go wrong. There is always a place for that unexpected kiss, and a little flirtation goes a long way. Be creative and experiment with romance and emotional affection to see what makes him feel better.

  When I walk by her in the kitchen, I often kiss her on the back of her neck and give her a little squeeze as I walk by. As you know, this is a two-way street.

- Belief in His Capabilities

  Most men believe it's important for them to protect and provide for those they love. So let your man know that you believe in his talents and skills. Be supportive of him.

- Respect

  The way you present yourself says a lot about the person you are. The way you dress to accentuate your body is nothing new, nor is it disrespectful. But this isn't what we are going to discuss here.

  In our twenty-first-century society, we have this what is called social media, and it is basically your resume for men. Where you go, what you say, who you are with—it reflects on you as an individual.

  Truthfully speaking, men don't want someone who is everywhere, doing everything with everyone. Often an old friend of mine sends me these pictures of outstanding looking women, but they are all topless. I wouldn't want to have my gal all over the Internet. Little boys who want the popular girl might, but real men don't play those games.

  You can't respect a man if you don't respect yourself.

  Most men prefer women who stay home reading a book or baking apple pies, as opposed to getting drunk with her friends on the weekend. We prefer the one whose life is kept more low-key because it makes her more intriguing.

- Confidence

  Has anyone told you that life is difficult? If you don't know it yet, every day is a struggle to get through. A confident woman by one's side is key to pursuing the man's dreams.

  One will find that a woman who loves herself, regardless of her own flaws, will love a man for all of his flaws. Beyond loving you, she will knock down the doors of resistance and reach for the stars for her man. This is what he is looking for.

  Men find something sexy about a confident woman, and it has nothing to do with looks. To be truthful, men don't notice every one of your flaws—you know, the ones you spend hours at the mirror pointing out to yourself.

It has been suggested that women are more committed simply because they have laser focus and can zero in on a problem or issue. With these women, failure isn't a choice.

It has been found that a woman who is willing to push forward to be the best mother to her children or have a successful career is one who will strive for a successful relationship. When things get tough for these women, they won't quit and walk away. If they lack ambition, however, odds are the result will look a bit different.

It is found that aspiring people usually figure out how to make things work.

- Humility
  When searching for a life partner, humble people focus their energies outward. This posture by a woman becomes very attractive to a man.

We find that humble women exude compassion for others and put others' happiness before their own. Women do this in such a way that it often brings them peace and protection.

Some Tips for Older Women

It is kind of sad but true: older gentleman have more issues with sex than women of about all ages. Therefore, their dealing with this issue may be the most valuable. It is not necessary to give up on something that is enjoyable by both sexes, but at the same time, one can be disappointed, and that is heartbreaking. This can be so disappointing that both parties could walk away saddened. Remember, it is not their fault; by and large, they want to make you happy. My philosophy is, "Happy wife, happy life."

So what can be done? Many men of all ages may not be open to talking about their erection problems. Erectile dysfunction can vary with age, but it doesn't come automatically with age. The dysfunction is not a normal part of aging. It is clearly an issue associated with other health issues.

- Women can help herself and her mate by talking about ED and learning something about it together. If you really care about you partner, this can rejuvenate your relationship and sex life, because it can die off over the years.
- Together, learn about various causes and alternatives, from pills to various foods and injections.
- Extra pounds can have a toll on your sex life, so encourage your man to work out with you. I used to swim as my second wife ran around the track at our retirement community.
- Remember that you aren't just helping him. Besides the sex angle, you are helping to improve your own heath.
- Cholesterol levels and diabetes both can lead to erection issues. Waist sizes over forty inches are more likely to increase problems with erections. Quitting smoking will be a benefit in reducing erectile dysfunction.

- Women and men can get involved in hand massages, and fellatio can be one of the cornerstones to great sex. This relationship can provide both men and women pleasure.
- The key here is to enjoy a good relationship. It must be a partnership between man and woman, working together to please one another. Part of this pleasure comes from good communication both ways. It is going to take both physical and emotional adjustments, but once you master the techniques, you'll be on the trail to mutually fulfilling lovemaking and happiness for the rest of your lives. One of the biggest keys is working and loving together.

I hope we are all adults here, and this is simply nature. Talking about sex is a win-win for all of us, so let's act like adults.

Talking to a very respected doctor in the field of ED and prostate cancer is a good idea for men of nearly all ages, but particularly for men over fifty. Radiation treatment is very successful, and there are other options that you can enjoy together to have a happy life.

Key to His Heart

First Date Preferences

We can say that women and men complement each other. Yes, on a basic level, your feminine qualities are what has attracted him, and you are moved by this masculine quality that attracts you to him. However, of the many ways men and women think differently, this is one of the favorites.

Generally, you will find that women will agonize over finding an outfit that is in style and trendy for their first date. In contrast, men are very often behind in recognizing women's trends, and they do not find them that important.

> This may mean that what you are wearing may send confusing signals to his brain if it does not automatically trigger a familiar feminine style at an unconscious level of evaluation. It is your feminine qualities that he sees, and these are what are attractive to him.

If you ask him after a date what you were wearing, you will be astonished at how little importance it has to him. You may find that only one thing will stand out in his mind.

Anything that accentuates your womanly qualities in a relaxed and comfortable way will be attractive to him.

You will find that the simpler and less fussy the patterns and cuts of your clothes, the more likely he is to have a positive first impression of you. Your clothing will not be busy distracting him from the simple elegance of your womanly figure.

Also, it is interesting to note the difference between men and women. Men aren't interested in learning about you on a first date. If you ask him what he thinks about the date, he is far more likely to give you a statement about what it feels like to be in your presence.

But women will more often respond to a friend's question with more details, like his occupation, or the number or sisters and brothers that he has. He will be more impacted by the emotions you generate in him—in man-speak, what it felt like to hang out with you.

You will find that men are more "here and now" when it comes to relationships. They do much less plotting and planning about the future of a relationship than women.

Also, men are far less likely to read into details and anticipate what those details mean about you. You will find if a man senses you are happy, that will go a long way toward creating a positive feeling to his interactions with you on that first date.

The Plan

I would like you to try to do this as honestly as you can. I would like you to develop two types of men here. One is Mr. Perfect. Now, I would ask you to set your parameters as honestly as you can. Make two columns at the top, and we are going to identify them as follows. Of course, you have the first column identified, Mr. Perfect, and the second column will be Mr. Excitable.

Mr. Perfect vs. Mr. Excitable

Six feet three plus vs. five feet nine
Sport figure vs. Average build
Long and wavy hair vs. Must have hair
Big brown eyes vs. Be able to see
Gourmet cook vs. Can make breakfast
Master's degree, doctor, or lawyer vs. A good job
Owns a home vs. Will buy you a nice home

Comfortable family vs. Divorced and broken home
Mixed religions in family vs. Same religious family
Father works for Dog pound
All members of the family go to family farm for Fourth of July
In secondary education or higher
Enjoys softball, dodgeball
Family travel out of the country once a year
Picnics at the park,
Drag racing
Enjoys or plays music, dancing, the arts, square dancing
Enjoys ribs and fried chicken,
Favorite foods are Kobe beef, lobsters

I want you to work on an honest review and real profile. If you want to use what others think of you, ask them to be truthful. Here are some things that I would like you to add. If you really like to go boating and have done so in the past, do not suggest this if you are not interested in being on a boat, and certainly. Don't suggest that you will enjoy helping him bait his fish if you never have done so. As I may have said, I am not a big hunter, but I do like to hunt wild hogs to help farmers and ranchers. You may or may not know that these animals do tens of thousands of dollars in damage to ranches and farms every year. I also have been in the NRA for over fourteen years, and I shoot or train up to two days a week. It used to be four days per week and one evening of tactical training. Now, I would enjoy having a female partner to go with me and shoot with me for company, and I would help train her.

If you really enjoy football, you can use this, or basketball or car racing. But if you put this down just to attract a fella, your guy is going to discover that you are bored, and he may look for a nice gal elsewhere. If you are telling the truth, you can simply be yourself. Pick something that you both enjoy, or find another guy.

For example, I like to horseback ride, go to the fair, go to a gun show, and watch a good science fiction movie. You are not going to find the right guy you are compatible with by trying to get into something that is not your cup of tea. Develop a list for yourself and compare it to the gentlemen you are trying to date.

I believe you don't have to like or dislike everything your partner does. For example, on one of the dating sites, it was not easy, and one way or another I met on the phone, in person, or via text more than four hundred women. Some were tall, some were short, and after reading almost every description, I believed some were a match. But they didn't think so. Some were Democrats, and because I wasn't, they didn't want to get to know me better. A few were vegetarians. I like my steak, and some would not date me because of what I eat. I don't care what you eat; a relationship is much more than your diet.

I really care for my girlfriend, and we often try to go to each other's restaurants. The place has something for both of us, and sometimes she will try something close to what I like, and sometimes I try to have something close to what she likes. But a loving relationship is more than a drumstick. She likes a little wine, but I rarely drink wine. We kind of enjoy the same movies. We are individuals with many likes and dislikes. This is what makes us different from one another. And these are what make up what we like and want in our individual relationships.

Now, I like tall women, but over the years, I have dated a nice lady who was as short as five feet. Sometimes, what we say is not what we do, and there are other overriding factors. I really like blonde hair, but I married a brunette and a blonde, and today I care for another blonde.

It is going to take a wiser man than me, but I believe there are some mysterious factors that we must consider. Can we make a mistake? I am sure we can. There are internal and external factors, and sometimes it is extremely difficult, if not impossible, to know what is right or wrong. If this wasn't true, there wouldn't be so many divorces.

What Do Older Men Want from Women in Bed?

This information is going to vary from gentleman to gentleman. By and large, men are not perfect, but this should give you some idea.

- They would like a woman who is confident and comfortable in her own skin. Please don't complain about something that you cannot accomplish, like any imperfections. We don't care if your breasts aren't perfectly firm and pert, if you have stretch marks, or if your skin is starting to wrinkle. Confidence is sexy.
- Know what turns you on. There is nothing sexier (in either partner) than someone who really knows what gets them excited and is willing to own it. There are lots of ways to own it.
- A woman who is realistic about sex. This is also true for what turns on mature women, by the way. Porn is great for entertainment if that's your thing, but it's problematic because it is poor a model for what actual sexual pleasure looks like for most people, particularly as you get older. It is not realistic to think that people can keep at it for endless hours or do it at the drop of a hat, and it's not usually all that pleasurable anyway. Get real.
- An older gentleman prefers women who don't fake it. He would like a gal who is honest enough to say that she is satisfied even if she didn't climax. Nothing is worse for a man's ego than discovering that his woman has been faking her pleasure. Be vulnerable enough to be real about that. If you're having difficulty, be honest and ask for what you need. Get some help to figure out what's causing the barrier. You deserve that for yourself.
- It is not all about sex. You will find that as men mature, they are interested in more than just a sexy body. A sexy brain also turns them on. This can be said for both sexes. Someone who has developed their own opinions and ideas, can articulate them clearly, and isn't always buried in her cell phone is also attractive.
- What we're looking at is honesty. Be willing to be real and vulnerable. Men really want to connect, but they do it a little

differently than women. If you don't know this already, mature men like all kinds of sex, depending on their mood. Yes there are personal preferences, and it also depends on their energy level and their innate sex drive. Sometimes they will enjoy sweet lovemaking, and sometimes they like down-and-dirty sex. It's all good. But you can ruin a good time when you are not willing to bring your true self to the plate. Try to always be there.

Remember that men in their fifties and older may not be as virile and energetic in the bedroom as they once were. Because of this, a vote of confidence or a pat on the back will be appreciated. If an older gentleman makes you feel good, don't be afraid to be loud about it. Be clear that what he is doing makes you feel great. Many older men (and even younger ones) would agree that telling a man what feels good is a turn-on. Take the time to tell him what he is doing is wrong. If you are somewhat shy about verbalizing your erotic emotions, moaning works and groaning is effective.

You will find that older men in bed are different from what younger men expect. They have more experience—as they say, a little older and a little wiser—and they have a better idea of what they want to enjoy. Just like other aspects of a relationship, as you grow older, you have a better idea of what does and doesn't work for you. Listen to your partner, speak to him about what you want, and find your way together. You both will appreciate the experience.

Tips for Younger Woman Who Would Like to Date Older Men

Many women find that dating men who are younger means they are very immature, only want sex, and don't know how to treat a lady well, and spend most of their time hanging out with their boys. If this is the case, maybe it is time to seek other opportunities and start dating older gentlemen. Even if it's only for a short time, this experience may give you invaluable insight. However, one you have had this experience with a mature relationship, you may decide to never go back to younger guys. Or at the least, you will be better prepared to choose more wisely when it comes to picking the right guy next time. Before you go off to the nearest bar or dating site, look at some tips to help you find a new knight.

- **Make sure he is a good fit.**
  Try to make sure he is a good fit, him and not the other way around. You may feel that you have to fit into his world because he's older, wiser, and set in his ways. By doing this, you're doing yourself a disservice. If you're not compatible, accept it and move on. You're too young to settle for someone who isn't right for you.

- **Don't be a trophy.**
  You will find that some older men will chase younger women as a way of making themselves feel younger, or to stroke their own ego by bagging "hot" young things. Don't assume that because he is older, he is going to be different than younger guys when it comes to using women as sex objects. You need to protect your heart and self-worth by jumping into sex or accepting expensive gifts too quickly. You don't want to wake up some morning and realize you are living in his house, driving his corvette, and using credit cards that are in his name, and he's having you there only

for sex. Basically, you are his prostitute, and I am sure this isn't going to sit well with you.

- **Don't assume he's going to use you**.
  Unfortunately, many women believe that men only want one thing, to have sex, and so there is a continuous flow of women in and out of their bedroom. This is not true. Most guys really would like to have a good relationship with balanced goals and both sides working out issues. Most men, like women, are complementary rather than supplementary. (They have talents in areas where the other person may be lacking. There can be assets like good sex, does laundry, good cook, dresses well for parties, and manages finances. You should know the difference.

- **Know your worth.**
  No, it is more than just knowing it. Make it clear that you are of equal worth to the guy. Then he will accept the fact, and his worth can rise to equal yours. This is what equality is all about: a balance.

- **Avoid the jealous type.**
  In contrast, a man who is somewhat jealous means you can almost count on him working hard to keep you. This may not be what you want. But aren't you looking for a committed relationship? If you are not, then don't select a jealous guy. However if you want to be committed, then you don't have to worry about a little bit of jealousy. Your job is to learn how to better channel through better communication.

- **Don't try to be his children's mother.**
  Here's the thing: the kids already have a mother. At this point, you are not playing house. You need to realize that these are real people's lives. Think how you might feel if some young gal came on the scene to take your place.

- **Be ready for his baggage.**
  One thing you can almost be assured of is that most of us will have some baggage, and as we get older, we are nearly assured that

we are going to gain more. Be sure that you know what you are getting into before you bite the bullet.

- **Do yourself a favor: respect his ex-wife.**
  Most of the time, you are going to find that she is not your competition. You must know that he has been down this road before. Here's the thing: if she is an ongoing part of his life, you really don't want to be there. It is best that you do your part to be friendly with her, because she can make your life a living hell. However she can also be the best resource for learning who this guy is. She has known him for some time. She may be his best judge of his character. But at the same time, there may be some bias to her observation, and at the same time you may not want this trouble in your life.

Older Gentlemen

1. Children—His and Yours

There are two things to consider here: his children, and your potential children. First, let's discuss his. You will find as a man gets older, it becomes increasingly likely that he will have fathered some children along the way. If he is a father, these children will take up his time, whether they live with him or he spends his weekends with them. You will probably need to be prepared to be lower on his list of priorities sometimes, even if his children are grown-ups. You might be fine with this, but it's important to carefully consider it.

As for your potential children, if he has children already, does he want any more? If he doesn't, are you prepared to sacrifice your desire for children to find love? The last thing you should do is enter the relationship thinking, "I'll change his mind." You most probably won't, and it's a huge gamble. It is important to talk everything through because these are issues that won't go away.

2. His Mindset

Meeting someone later in life means they're more likely to have become set in their ways. Their ideas about the way the world should work will be fully formed, and it's very unlikely they'll change. We're not saying older men will be completely inflexible, but you shouldn't think you can change their ways once you're in a relationship.

3. Cultural References

We use cultural references to express who we are and where we've come from. If you find it odd that his favorite bands are Genesis and ELO, then you will need to decide whether you can get used to that, or whether you will feel increasingly isolated. Also remember that older men will have the same dilemma with any references you make that may make them feel old and distant from you.

4. His Health

You are going to find that the older you are, the more health problems you get. He may be forty-five and fit now, but when you're reaching middle age, he might be classed as a senior citizen and will most likely suffer from ill health. These problems will become yours too if you're to have a happy, understanding relationship.

5. His Desire for Sex

It's generally considered that women peak sexually between twenty-five and forty, whereas men peak between eighteen and twenty-five. It doesn't take a genius to work out the difference there, but you should bear in mind that everyone is different. Also, though your older man might lack the sex drive of a twenty-two-year-old, he will likely have the experience to put many younger men to shame.

6.   His Energy Levels

Just as his health will possibly deteriorate, your older man's energy levels will also drop over time. Yes, we all know some lazy men our own age, but older men might need to go to bed earlier than you, and they're probably not going to find late-night house parties very appealing. Then again, you might not either, so you might be perfect for each other.

7.   Your Bank Balances

If you're relatively young and single, chances are you have a bit of disposable income. Yet, while your older man probably earns a decent salary, you should remember that he might have more serious financial commitments than you.. While you want to go on a last-minute trip to Europe, he might prefer to put the money into his pension or spend it on his children Education.

8.   Spontaneity

This goes hand in hand with point number two. The older you are, the more you know what you like and dislike, and the less likely you are to try new things or act in a spontaneous way. This is not to say that you get boring as you get older; it's simply that responsibilities get in the way. For a long weekend away, you just need to pack a bag and go, whereas he needs to make sure his children are cared for, and he must square things at work and take care of the dogs. On the plus side, you may find the stability in your life comforting and reassuring.

A Little Review

I have touched on this before, but it is very important. Many gentlemen would agree with me, but I am going to suggest that you get yourself some very current photos, and I mean good ones. If necessary, have at least one taken by a professional photographer. Dress up somewhat formally and involve some of your favorite activities, especially if you are going to promote the fact that these are some of your interests. If you were selling your house for top dollar, would you want the potential buyer to see its best assets? All these pictures are what you are selling. You are the prize that we men are looking for. One of the biggest mistakes is that photos need to be timely. If you are fifty years of age, men want to see you as you are now. You need a photo from about the waist up. I don't know about

others, but I would like to see your face and hair, and maybe a full-length picture too. Also, I like to see how you look in a dress. There was a gal I met a few months ago, and she looked like a bag lady. I am sorry, but this is true.

Some of you gals are missing an opportunity here. Who suggested that you put up no picture? To make a point, when a big firm is selling cars or other products, it puts an ad in the newspapers and on TV and billboards. Do they put up pictures of blank screens? No! They try to put out photos of the best-looking cars they have, or the best thing that is pleasing to the eye. You should too!

I was checking one of the sites today—yes, I am still getting inquiries, mostly out of my dating range, though I am not presently looking; I am in the process of testing a relationship. I get three women to take a look at, so what is the first thing that I see? Well, all three had a generic silhouette of a female (the default image), and that was the first thing I saw. Second, they were over two hundred miles from my location. I believe that I have a realistic dating range of around fifty miles, so I try to give each one a nice message, but by and large, I am not interested in them for two reasons: the nonphoto and the distance. I am trying to be fair to the both of us. I don't have a real statistical number on this, but I bet you dollars to donuts that the rejection rate due to not having a photo is more than 20 percent, and this is by guys who might be interested in you, not the scammers or players.

[Don't do this. We would like to see you, not the pool, the goat, your you're your flowers, or your grandkids.

Weird Stories—True, but Not the Date You Are Looking For!

These stories are based on actual dates.

1. I met this guy, and he seemed okay. We had been talking online, and he was nice and normal. He also seemed to have a good job and was funny and intelligent. I met him for a drink. His first question upon sitting down at the table was whether I was up for anal sex. I bypassed the question and sat there watching this guy drink his body weight in drinks. The next thing I knew, he was crying and talking about his ex-girlfriend. I got him out of the bar and walked him home, and suddenly he was throwing up down my shoulder. This was about a year and a half ago, and to this day he is still texting me. The only thing I can say here is try to watch for better signs. You might need to spend more time talking to him on the phone before you meet him for a drink.

2. I met this guy, and he seemed decent. He asked me to go to a movie with him, and this seemed like a reasonable request. We went to this film, but he kept talking about my feet, telling me how beautiful and sexy they were. I thanked him. Later during the movie, he asked me if he could suck my toes, I said, "Hell no." Later, I noticed that he dropped something on the floor, but he put the toes of my crossed legs in his mouth, so I kicked him in his face. I excused myself to the ladies room, but instead I walked out of the theater and left him there.

3. I met this guy on a dating site, and I was surprised that we really hit it off. After we hung out a few times, he came over to my place with a bottle of wine, and we watched a movie on TV. Now, he wasn't supposed to stay over that night, but he lived about an hour away. I kind of live in the county with lots of trees, and it is hilly with some

curved roads. He decided that he was going to stay instead of driving home. I was irritated. He did ask, but he just assumed it was okay.

The best part of the night was just before I went to bed (he was staying on the couch), he told me I should change my pad before I went to bed because I could get toxic shock syndrome. He proceeded to argue with me for over ten minutes about whether or not I should change my pad. He said he was an EMT and had a sister, so he "knows all about this stuff." My argument was I had been a virgin for twenty years. Needless to say, he went home the next morning, and I never saw him again.

4. I was chatting with this fellow on a dating site for some time, and it seemed to go well. Then he asked me out to dinner, so I said, Why not? But it turned out to be one of the most awkward and uncomfortable nights of my life. We spent our time attempting to have this disjointed conversation, and at the end of the evening we simply said good night and parted ways. I thought, This is the end of it. But approximately seven months later, I received this message on my computer roughly saying, "This is Larry's brother. This is going to sound odd, but Larry is in jail for a few months, and I know that he would like to get a letter or two from you. His address is … Can you please write to him?"

5. For some time I was having very pleasant conversations with this gentleman online. After a few hours of friendly conversation with "Henry," the talk turned 180 degrees. First, out of this mouth comes, "Where do you work? Because you look familiar to me." He then said, "You look like this gal on an amateur porn video I have." I knew this was not possible. The next thing he asked me nearly blew my mind: "You don't mind if I jerk off while we continue the conversation, do you?" I put down my phone so hard that you could hear it in Philadelphia. But this wasn't the end. This guy sent me all these messages on the computer asking me to help him orgasm by telling him that what he did was okay and normal. Apparently, he had issues and had a hard time finishing without someone telling him it was okay to do what he was doing. I never responded.

6. I was talking with this guy on one of the dating sites, and he sounded kind of charming. We seemed to be getting along okay. Then he came up with a story that he needed some help getting into the United States. I say, "Oh? How come? And what kind of help do you need?" He said to me, "Well, I need someone to marry me, and I would give you $1,250 if you would, but the marriage is only for a year." It seemed he was from the Middle East and wanted to become an American citizen. I told him no. He couldn't understand why I would say no and said that there were several women out there who would do it for half the money. I said, "That may be true, but that's not me!"

7. I met "John" online, and I have to say we hit it off on our first date. We were a couple just a few weeks later. We had gone on about six dates, and by this time he knew where I lived. That was when it started to get strange. He started not returning my phone calls, so after a week I stopped calling. Not long after this, I was looking out the window of my apartment, and there he was parked a few houses down the street. He was in the truck with another person. Then in an hour or so, they drove off. A few days later, I saw the truck again, but parked in another location. Naturally I got upset and freaked out. They left in about an hour. This time I called the police, and e-mailed him, telling him that I had called the cops. I demanded that he take me out of his dating book, and I told him this was goodbye, so long, and farewell!

8. I was new to this dating site, but I did meet this gentleman about my age. He seemed nice, and through our conversations, he sent me this text: "Pizza and anal?" Now, thinking he is nuts, I sent back something about how I would definitely take the pizza but would pass on the anal. He replied with, "As long as I can suck your toes, we're golden." That was the last time I communicated with this guy!

9. I was somewhat new to this one site—I am not going to say which one. I received this message: "I came across your profile recently, and I was really quite enamored by such an articulate profile, and beautifully done. I would have to have to kick myself If I didn't take the time to ask, so I was wondering if you would accept meeting me for an

engagement of witty talk between the two intellectuals. Of course this get-together may start off as purely platonic, but it is very possible that my sexual desire will guide us to a cohesive unity down a more erotic path, and that could include, but is not limited to, passionate make-out sessions under a starlit sky with dry humping, some fondling one another, and exploring uncharted sexual positions." Do I have to say that I never responded?

Staying Safe Online

When it comes to online safety, particularly when it comes to dating and companionship, I know a little about it. I have been on about four sites and worked with and dated around four hundred women. I didn't go out with that many, but I talked to that many, dated a fair number, and e-mailed and corresponded with a good number. There is a site called Stitch, and as I understand, it is the only companionship site in the world that insists on verification for its members. They do a lot of things behind the scenes to ensure that Stitch is free of scammers and fraudsters, which most dating sites simply don't do. Ask any of their members, and they'll tell you this extra focus on safety creates an environment that's unlike anything they've found elsewhere. But as I said, I have not used this site yet.

It also means you are going to get some extraordinary insights into the sorts of things that scammers, fakes, and fraudsters will try to do to get money (or worse) from their intended victims. Given many of these things apply not only to dating sites but also to all sorts of online social networks, here are some practical tips that might help you. Think about these tips when communicating with anyone you don't know online, and particularly if you are trying to find a companion.

The Danger Is Real

Before we jump into some of the guidance, these issues are not made up. The danger from scammers online is very real. I know because I have had seven attempts in the last two years.

Not only does one report after another highlight how many people are being duped by scammers every year, but I have had a number from various sites share a few of their stories, and I am going to share them with you. Some did lose money, but others lost jewelry and time. Some have had their hearts cracked a little.

Here is a story about "Mary," a dating site member who lost close to ten thousand dollars to a scammer from Ghana. She wanted to truly understand how the scammers worked.

After being stung, she was so upset that she went back to night school and trained as a private investigator. Her specialty? You guessed it: cybersecurity, with a focus on fighting scammers.

This was Mary's way of getting back at those who had hurt her. She shared dozens of stories of men and women who had lost far more than she had to sophisticated online scams. Some victims had ended up in jail after being unwittingly duped into committing crimes themselves.

Most amazing were the images of scammers boasting about their exploits online, flashing photos of the cash they had stolen, and sharing tips with fellow scammers on online forums and Facebook groups. Even if only one person in a thousand falls for their scams, it's still worth their time.

In my case, one of the gals asked me to send her money to pay off creditors so she could fly over from where she lived to visit me. This was another thing: in the beginning, it was suggested that she had access to an aircraft and could fly herself, but the closer we got, and before she tried to spring the "send me money" bit, she was going to fly from Cincinnati. Or that was the story. No, I wasn't going to finance her creditors or pay any airfare. First, I had never seen her or spent any time with her, and I had no idea who she was. Besides, Cincinnati and me in Dallas? This was not an arrangement made in heaven! Could you imagine the cost for traveling just to get to know someone, even if it was a real relationship in the making?

One young lady wanted me to pay for a machine, to help her in her small business. Do you know how to say *goodbye* in Japanese? Sayonara.

Over Fifty? You Need to Be Extra Careful

Unfortunately, if you are over fifty, then you need to be more careful. Statistics show that not only seniors are more likely to have fallen for an online scam, but they are more likely to be targeted, and when they lose money, they lose more than their younger peers.

The Good News

If everything above makes you want to avoid dating or going online altogether, there is good news. It's not hard to stay safe if you follow a few simple, common-sense guidelines. In many cases, it's simply enough to remember to behave the same way online as you would in the real world.

You'd think more than once before getting into a complete stranger's car, wouldn't you? I'm pretty sure you wouldn't give them your bank or credit card details either.

If you wouldn't do either of these things in the everyday world, then it should be easy to stay safe on those dating sites, as long as you understand how to play the game and use your common sense from the real world. Translate that common sense to the world of online dating.

The Biggest Risks

A few words here before we take a look at some into some guidelines. We are dealing with two different types of risks you might be facing when you venture into dating online:

- The first risks that you might face are from a predator on a dating site or online, including being defrauded for your money, savings, or identity. Another gal wanted me to help her stay in the United States and get her deceased husband's money. She said she was from Holland, had a lot of money, and was willing to do just about anything, including marrying me and living happily ever after. I had to help her get to Fort Worth, Texas; pay her bus fare from South Texas; help her with a lawyer; marry her; and more.

To be honest, at this point we were talking a few thousand dollars, but it could have gone from there. But the next morning, I provided all this information to the police as fast as I could. I still got called for a few more days by this gal.

- The second risks you face from a predator are in person, for example being sexually assaulted by someone who meets you for a day or picks you up for at a restaurant or at your home.

Both types of risks are a concern, but when it comes to people on dating sites, the greatest risk by far is online threats. It is estimated a senior's chances of experiencing abuse in today's world is one in a thousand. Of course, if you are that one, it can be very costly and painful.

This may surprising you, but the reason is very clear.

1. **The rewards are high.**
   Scammers have been able to steal hundreds of thousands of dollars from one or more victims. If you're an unemployed person in a low economic country, this opportunity looks quite good.

2. **The risks are low for those entering this vocation.**
   The risk is low for the online scammer, and the opportunity is high. You will find that law enforcement does not do much, and the scammers put themselves at very little risk. The ones who meet you in person face a greater risk of getting caught, however.

3. **It's easy to work in a wide area.**
   When you are doing an in-person crime, it doesn't scale very well because the criminal can only work or deal with one victim at a time. Online crime lets criminals target thousands of victims from the safety of their own homes. That's important when it comes to fraud, because professional scammers may have to work a high number of potential people before they get one to fall for a scam.

4. **It's easy to impersonate someone else online.**

> The key to most online dating scams is the ability of scammers to pretend that they are someone else. Often the scam involves a story about traveling aboard, getting into trouble, and asking the victim to wire them money.

Another one of my gals I was involved with for a short time told me that she was some kind of self-employed entrepreneur—in the rug business or something. I got this phone call from her, and she said she was in trouble. She needed more money because her check didn't clear, or she had trouble with the process, and she was buying these items in Dubai or someplace in the Middle East. She needed this cash to cover a shortfall. Of course I said I couldn't do that, and that was the end of it. But these scams are out there every day.

5. The older users are far less likely to experience the physical assault problem. Here is one area where being a little older makes us a little safer. Usually the sexual violence is far less likely to happen to us older persons. The fact is we are about twenty-three times less likely to experience any sexual assault. Now, if you are over fifty, your greatest risk is facing someone you meet.

6. For the most part, this is really only feasible online. It's extremely difficult for a nineteen-year-old scammer in Ghana to impersonate a sixty-five-year-old account executive in Chicago in person!

I'm not saying you don't need to exercise caution when meeting a stranger for a date—you absolutely should. But if you are over fifty, statistically speaking, the greatest risk you face in the online dating world comes when you are dealing with someone online.

With this in mind, I've focused my guidance on how to keep yourself safe online when using online dating sites, and most of the tips below relate to online safety.

Without further ado, here are our top fifteen tips for staying safe on online dating sites.

1.   Look them up (and embrace your inner stalker)

You need to remind yourself that you know absolutely nothing about the person you've just met, apart from what they've said on their profile. Fortunately, there are a number of things you can do to get more information about them, including:

- Find them on Facebook (but don't become friends — see below!). Gather as much information you can to reassure yourself that they are who they say they are. Do you have mutual friends? If so, ask your friends about them. How many friends do they have? How authentic are their posts? Are their posts consistent with who they say they are and where they live?
- Find them on LinkedIn and do the same
- Do a reverse image search on their profile pictures. If you use Chrome as your browser, this is absurdly easy to do: just right-click on the image and choose "Search Google for Image". If not, just open images.google.com in your browser, click the photo icon and paste in the image you want to search. Many scammers use images stolen from public profiles and will show up on multiple sites under different names. If they do, stay away!
- Google them! You can often find people simply based on a location, a first name, and some of the basic information they provide on their profile
- Do it the old-fashioned way: just ask them for some information that you could use to verify that they are who they say they are. If they say they work at your local library, for example, give the library a call and ask to speak to them ... it can be that simple!

2.   Look out for the warning signals

No matter how long you've known someone online, you should be on the lookout for any of the following warning signals:

- Someone who says they live locally, but are currently traveling abroad for work or vacation
- Asking for money or donations

- Any form of solicitation or spam
- Asking your address to send you flowers or gifts
- Asking you for personally identifying information
- Hard luck stories (e.g. sudden and unexpected medical expenses for their kids)
- Similarly, stories that are too good to be true … such as a great business opportunity — if only they had some money
- Asking you to get off the dating site and communicate via a different chat system
- Early and enthusiastic declarations of love — let's be realistic, if you met someone in the real world and started saying they loved you after a couple of conversations you'd be suspicious, wouldn't you?
- Anything that feels a little off kilter — such as getting basic information about your area wrong, as though they were learning about it from the Internet, poor spelling and grammar that isn't consistent with who they claim to be, using an international phone number, etc
- Not being willing to meet in person

3.   Don't give out your personal information, not even your email address

This one is a no-brainer but is easy to get wrong. Do you know how many cases of identity theft start with an email address? If you don't use strong passwords a thief will often be able to hack into your email once they know a few basic bits of information about you, by using the password recovery process that most email systems provide. Once they have your email address, the next step is to use it to get the login to more important information, such as your bank account.

The same goes for address information, social security numbers, postal addresses, etc. Never give out any personal information to someone you have only met online.

4.   Verify they match their profile

Remember the example I gave earlier about the scammer from Ghana impersonating the executive in Chicago? The sooner you are able to check that the person at the other end of the internet connection simply *looks* like their profile, the quicker you will have eliminated 95% of the scammers out there.

The simplest way to do this is to meet in person, of course, and we've got some advice about doing this further down on the list below.

But you don't even need to wait to do this: The Internet now provides a number of tools for having a video call with someone which don't require you to hand out your Skype ID or email address.

A favorite is Appear (appear.in), which lets you set up an instant, private video chat with someone for free, without giving out any personal information. It's super-simple and doesn't require any software to install.

Of course, if you can get them to chat to you via Appear and they *do* look like their profile then it's no guarantee they are trustworthy, but it definitely does mean you've reduced your risk significantly. So this can be very helpful.

5.   Meet in person

Even better than a video chat is to meet in person, of course. If you do this, just remember that the first meeting isn't really a "date" for either of you; it's much more of a verification session about whether you are comfortable enough to go on that first date. So you need to be careful with what you say.

With that in mind, I would recommend starting with a daytime coffee meeting with a reasonably strict time limit — that way it's not a surprise when you decide it's time to leave. Meeting in a neutral public place that's not close to your home is always advisable, and if you're able to do it at a group event then even better ... I know we did say the main risk is online but it's still worth being careful!

Given 99.9% of scammers in the world live in cities other than yours, the fact that someone simply agrees to have coffee with you in the first place is a great sign. And once you've met them, you'll have a much better idea that they are who they say they are, and whether you might like to go on that first date or not.

One thing I would definitely caution against: stay away from drinking alcohol on that first meeting. I don't know anyone whose judgment got *better,* after a couple of glasses of wine or something stronger!

6.   Don't connect on Facebook

I talked about this earlier, but it's reviewing, there are a great many items of personally identifiable information about you from your Facebook profile. If you are there, more than likely your photo is there too, and information; you, your kids names; maybe your pet's names (often used as passwords!); I have to tell you, I am there, my deceased wife, and more. This before I wised up.

So, you need to keep them away and out of your online life until they are well and truly a part of your real life.

7.   You will want to Stay local

Now if you're using a site like Stitch which offers specific protections for communicating with other persons in other countries around the world, we I am going to recommend getting involved with only with people who live in your City, town, or State As you can see this reduces the cuts the risk that you're going to be talking to someone who says they live in Canada but really they actually live in South Africa.

I remember one time, a few years ago, where, I was in a Business situation, and I was talking to this, gentleman with this strong accent, and he was trying to do business with us, and I could hear the Chickens in the background, so also be aware during your early conversations, or what you hear on the phone.

The next point,

Use only reputable, trusted sites

8. You are going to find a large number of dating sites available out there worldwide. With most being small, but there are more small, but highly specialized and in niches, and these are small, (dating for some for over 50, Religious, gun enthusiasts, farmers, Animal lovers, younger people, etc) and most don't have the resources, don't care, or desire, to ensure communities scammer-free. So your best bet is to stay with the Dating sites that care and do a good job of keeping their communities protected.

9. If there is any question, or some doubt, the best thing to do is delete. And report.

Now sometimes it will take a little work but report the profile to the administrator and then delete them from your computer. Don't stay long because their profile sounds smooth, or that they have developed a great connection with you. Some of the worst cases of scams involve a person that has discovered the scammer was a fraud but continues to correspond with the scammer, letting their emotions get in the way and throwing all caution to the wind in the quest for love.

So please don't go there and make the same mistake!

10. Beware of links and attachments

One of the things that you have to beware of are any links or attachments sent to you by someone you don't have any idea who they are, and have your doubts, this is one of the simplest, but highly successful cyber-attacks methods. When it comes it is designed to convince you to click on this attachment. The upside for you is that more than likely it isn't going to come from someone you meet for a date in person, but it *is* something sophisticated scammers do utilize.

11. Having a separate email address

Now if you are sticking to this guideline about not giving out your personal details then it is more than likely not important to worry much about this one.

However, if you are extra-paranoid, you will find it simple to set up a dedicated email address say (a Gmail account) that you are only going to use online for dating. This way you will have another level of security and that if the account is hacked, you are not at risk of losing any critical personal information, and it can't be used to gain access to any of your other accounts.

12. Use dedicated photos

Now, I know that I talk about having a good, attractive picture on your dating site, and one that shows you in a good light, but only place photos on your profile that you use for dating, and nothing else. This prevents scammers from using your picture (they know how to use Google Image Search too, to trace your profile back to you, and this way discover additional personal information about you from the Internet.

13. It is very important that you continually remind yourself that you have not met this person yet.

Get this in your mind, matter how long you've known someone online they are not real until they are sitting in front of you and this is still somewhat questionable. And if you have not really met this person in today's world — and haven't followed these recommendations and ideas, then you need to constantly remind yourself, "I really don't know this person yet", and you need to treat them that way.

If your date offers to pick you up in a car for the evening, ask yourself: if I was out for dinner or in a bar for the first time and a person asked me out or asked me to get in their vehicle would I do this, and of course the answer should be no!?

If they offer to take you on a tropical vacation, and you really didn't know this person, would you go? Ask yourself: would you do that with someone you haven't spent time with yet, or now really know them?

You wouldn't.

So do your homework, make sure you find out who they are. Do your research. Get a paper trail. Now that you have done this research, THEN, after you have done these precautions you might be able to, just remember…

14. Don't be TOO suspicious

So you may sound and seem really odd and paranoia, but it's important to remember you're on a dating site in order to connect with people. It is important not to seem too different and too suspicious of the people you meet. you're never going to trust anyone that you come across or meet. And at the same time, they are going to be at odds with you and see that there us something unusual with you, to the point they are not going to be interested in you either.

Not everyone is going to be perfect. Maybe they don't have a Facebook profile so you can't check them out online. Or maybe they ask for your phone number because they are trusting and just want to call you, not because they're a scammer.

At some point you need to make a judgment call about the person you're talking to. All we're saying is that you need to exercise a little bit of common sense.

15. Or … Just use Stitch

Of course, I can't end the article without mentioning what we think is the **BEST** way to stay safe on an online dating site: just join Stitch. No other site takes such care to ensure its members are who they say they are: all Stitch profiles go through multiple levels of verification check, to ensure our membership consists only of real, verified, individuals. On top of this, the community aspect of Stitch allows us to check on our members' behavior in ways that no other site can do.

Unfortunately, if you're under 50 you'll need to wait a few years before you can join: Stitch is only available to people over 50!

Try to use the suggestions on how to stay safe on online dating sites. Do you have safety tips of your own to share, or experiences with scammers on other dating sites? Let us know in the comments below!

What Can You Count On?

I have been on four sites, one or two for about a year or so, and I have dropped off one. You must decide how many sites and which ones you are going to keep active. They take time to have them work right for you, not to mention the cost. It is clearly a matter of economics. I have no idea which is best for me, let alone what is good or best for you. There are new ones coming out all the time. It will take a little time to learn how to manage each site because they are all a little different, but they are similar in the way they work. The first thing I suggest is once you have a handle on how to use the site, pick a simple password. In fact, today the new approach to passwords is "keep it simple." I am slowly moving in this direction myself because I have had too many passwords to remember. Have one or two good ones, or do what you will and use many. If I were to do it over, I would have one for all the sites that I am on, but it would be something I only know, like my mom's shoe size, how tall my father was, or my favorite dog at the time.

Yes, beauty is in the eye of the beholder, but we want to help in this case as best we can. It is safe to say you have an idea of the look of the guy you are looking for, and so does your guy. Give him the best job you can by providing him with that opportunity.

Do you want to join a dating site, or look like the Witches of Eastwick? Would you go fishing without a hook? If you go to a gunfight, don't take a knife. Therefore, look the best you can and provide the best photos you can. You might say it is expensive, and that may be true, but you have already invested in the site, so you should want to do your part to help the site work for you in the best way possible. Start with the best photo you can, and you may hold the future in the palm of your hand.

I am going to assume that some, if not most, of you gals have watched *The Bachelor*, and when you see a photograph of these gals, is the shot so far away you can't make out the person? Or if they are looking down, or is there a piece of the face missing? No, and that shouldn't be true of yours either. You should have the best smile too!

As a Younger Woman, Why Would I Want to Date an Older Man?

You will find that there are at least two sides to this phenomenon. There are many women seeking to build a relationship with older men. There are also others who look down on the May-December relationship. There may be legitimate reasons why these women seek out older men with whom to have a romantic relationship.

- The first question is, Why do women find these older men more desirable than their younger counterparts?

1. Older men by and large are more experienced and possibly cultured.

As they say, men are like wine and get better with age. Of course, they have more life experiences, at work in other relationships, and these experiences have given them life lessons to make their situation better than before. Older men are usually more mature and understand that things don't always happen the way they want them to, so they are more understanding and patient with their partners.

Older men know what they want, and they intend to go after it. They tend to be more confident and carry themselves very well, especially in public. Older gentlemen are generally better mannered. Because of their longevity, they tend to travel better, and they tend to know a lot of things about other cultures.

2. It is safe to assume the old gentlemen are more financially stable.

Most women are looking for men who are in a financial situation where they can support others financially.

This is not about being a gold-digger or social climber. It is often all about being realistic. When you are starting a family, it is important that the guy is able to provide a secure environment for his family. And an economically successful woman will not easily settle for an individual who makes less than she does.

One can pretty much assume that a typical young man in his late twenties will have less savings, less wealth, and fewer assets compared with what he'll have in twenty more years.

Of course, you will find people who will suggest that money isn't everything, and you can't buy love. However, there is a certain amount of income that you need to get by.

Older gentleman likely has assets as well as the funds to support his family. Therefore, women will go for men who have the financial ability to take care of them instead of someone who is just starting out in a career.

3. There is a good chance that old guys may be better in terms of pleasing and dealing with women.

It has been said to me that gentlemen have had their share of short-term and long-term relationships, so this gives them an advantage when it comes to handling a relationship. These men can refer to previous experience they have had to help them learn what women generally want and what makes women happy.

It is safe to say that generally they have had more exposure in bed too, and they can understand women a little better. Plus, they are more sensitive to the needs of their partner. Women generally can expect that older men have a good sense of humor.

4. More often you will find that older gentlemen are seeking serious relationships.

It has been found that gentlemen mature much slower than women, and normally men who are middle aged are mature than young men. This is when they now are seeking more stable and healthy relationships.

If you are tired of short relationships and immature ones, there is a good chance you will be more satisfied, plus it is likely a stabler relationship with an older guy than some young fellow in his late twenties. You will find that younger men as a rule are still wanting to explore and try different things before settling on something more serious.

5. As a rule, you will find older gentlemen have more sophisticated tastes.

    When it comes to the finer things in life like wine, food, beer, traveling, and clothing, these gentlemen will tend to go for sophistication. First, they have the income that allows them to buy them, and second, they know better quality when they see it.

    By and large, when it comes to food and drinks, quality does not always come with a high price. You don't always need to eat at a high-end restaurant to enjoy a good meal. An affordable place can be found that serves quality food at reasonable pricing, and the food just might be better.

    Older gentlemen are less likely to be less insecure about their position in life, so they don't need to go out and blow money on pricey meals. It goes without saying he generally knows what he wants.

    As for travel, you will find that older men tend to avoid tourist traps and are very happy to get away from the crowd. They like roaming around and are just as happy sitting in one spot where they can enjoy all the scenery at their own time and speed. Many older people are experienced travelers.

6. Because of their longevity, you can generally be assured that older gentlemen are good cooks.

It is safe to assume that older men can cook. I am not going to say that they are all amazing, but I have been around the kitchen enough that I know how to do more than boil water, and I am sure that a good number of men are in the same category. It has been said that many women find these cooks sexy, and this is great, though I don't think you are going to find me there anytime soon. But the other side of the coin is many younger guys have a hard time opening a can, let alone boiling water.

7. You will often find older gentlemen living a better, healthier lifestyle.

They are not out seeing how much beer they can drink through a plastic hose. Those days are over. Sure, they enjoy a good glass of wine or two, and maybe some of them smoke, but they generally know their limitations. Of course, this is not the case when they are having problems coping with their own issues, which is an exception because as we know, older gentlemen do a better job of handling their own issues because they are more mature than younger men.

You will often find that older gentlemen find time away from the office to get involved in things they enjoy doing. I find myself getting more involved in sports and handgun shooting over the last year, and until somewhat recently I did tactical training. I also hunt wild hogs. These older men do keep active away from their office. You will find these gentlemen spending money on their hobbies, like flying or working on their classic car or motorcycle, but not on stuff like gadgets and computer games, which seem to be popular with younger men. You may find these old guys are also involved in travel.

Older guys do understand the need to relax from time to time, and they are not motivated to be constantly pushing themselves like a lot of younger men do. These gentlemen will focus on a more laid-back approach.

8. The older gentlemen will be less likely to focus on the party.

> I have to say that I have enjoyed a good party a few times per year, but I never aligned myself with any of those so-called party animals. I am not much for crowds—in fact, I would prefer to walk across the street from a big party. You will generally find younger guy at parties, making a lot of noise and seeing how many bottles of beer they can drink. And yes, there is loud music too.
>
> I will let the cat out here, now that I am an older gentleman: I like to hear what the person I am with is saying. I generally didn't like the noise of parties, and I have had much of my hearing taken away by the military. I enjoy being with a nice woman, and because I am already hard of hearing, I don't like to miss what she is saying. I enjoy joking around and talking about my family, some of my experiences, her experiences, what we have in common, where we grew up, and background stories. I like to hear about what she enjoys doing. Many older men will talk about some politics, likes, and dislikes.

Older men can see the poor party patterns of younger guys. Often young men tend to focus on the poor lifestyle, which is often difficult to maintain—and worse, it is not good for their health. Of course, that can parallel their focus on their lifestyle. Instead, they tend to put most of their attention on their friends and being in social environments where all can be heard, with little if any privacy for anyone.

Summary

If you are a gal looking for some type of balance in your life, a family, a smoother lifestyle, or more security, then it can be wise to at least look at the many opportunities of dating older gentlemen. I am sure you can find a great guy closer to your age, but if any other areas that have been listed here gain your interest, it is to your benefit to look and do the math. Remember that it is your life and happiness, so it is up to you to get the best out of it.

The Reasons Women Date Older Men

I.   Most older men have more experience and culture. You are not going to see your man trying to sneak in the back door so they don't get caught by their father.

II.   Most are financially stable. Normally you will not find them asking you for money because they were foolish with their wallet and it was stolen.

III.   Older gentlemen are more likely to want to please you than a young guy.

IV.   Older guys are more likely looking for a serious relationship.

V.   They have a more sophisticated taste and will more likely be drinking out of a bottle than a hose when you meet them.

VI.   It is more likely that they can cook you a meal and not burn water.

VII.   Older gentlemen are usually living a healthier lifestyle, and they have given up all-night binges.

VIII. These gentlemen are past the partying stage that young guys are still in, making them more responsible.

IX.   Then there are those psychological and biological reasons that play, which manages to help the older man be more responsible.

So Just What Are You Looking for—a Younger Guy, a Gigolo, or a Caring Gentleman?

I ask this question of you, and if you don' t have an answer for me, this is a question that you have to ask yourself. In the short run a relationship might be fun, but more than likely it will be short. Is this what you want?

What am I talking about? Well, some weeks ago I was talking to a very old friend who is retired, married, and lives in this upscale retirement community in Arizona. We call him Vern. He told me, "You need to come over here. There are about 150 single women here, and with your background, you should be able to find one." Of course, my answer was, "That's good, Vern, but this is a long commute." One of your problems could be the same as mine: the commute. I have already discussed this at some length. To really get to know someone, you need to spend a lot of time with the person. In this case, the one thing you get to know is the highway. If I lived nearby, the outcome of any of my relationships could be different.

Vern went on to say many of these women in the Arizona retirement community were looking for younger men who could provide them with companionship on cruises that older gentlemen don't like because they get sick and have more physical issues. One thing he didn't tell me was how old these younger men were. I am seventy-eight, though I can often pass for a sixty something. Vern went on to tell me that these women were too.

I said I would try to talk to not only the guy but also the women to pick up pointers. I ran across this woman who told me that this information was not totally true. She said that she had gone on as many as thirty cruises, so I assumed that she had more experience than I did.

She told me that part of the information I got was true. Often these women were seeking younger men, but not for their money. Gals were buying these gigolos for their company, and they were willing to pay for their time for a one- or two-week fake romance. Then the young men would leave the women flat when the cruise was over. A more mature, sincere gentleman may be a little slower, but he is real (generally speaking). And it may cost you less from your heart as well as out of your pocket.

Now, shame on me and some of the other guys out there, because there are many of us who are looking for a real relationship. As you can see, I am assuming there are other gentlemen looking for the same thing, but it could cost you more than a cruise.

Problems Your Dad and Mom Didn't Face

Let us zero in on this for a little while. Yes, Mom and Dad did have some of the issues that we find today, but let's look at them closely.

First, there are new rules on how you meet. Did you know this? This includes where you go and who pays the bill, which are more flexible then back in Dad's time.

There is information on dating sites and apps that can expand your search for new places to go. You can find information on possible candidates that allows you to acquire valuable data on people before you meet them.

But at the same time, you will also find that dating today can be more challenging, complicated, and even dangerous. I have touched on this a little. There are things that Mom and Dad were never concerned with or had to deal with.

You can use social media to find good or not-so-good information on an individual. It is possible to find out about people's hobbies, the way they vote, and even what they had for breakfast.

Now, having this information may be good or bad, and it may be unfair to you and your potential date. All this information may cause you to have preconceived ideas and expectations as to how this date is going to go. You may already have some idea as to how this date is going to turn out, and you could be completely wrong. Often the first date is a lot of fun because you have a great deal of new things to talk about, sharing ideas and learning facts that you don't have to pretend that you didn't know.

Today, I find dating online with email, dating sites, Facebook, Instagram, Messenger, and numerous dating sites confusing, sometimes complicated, and even a little dangerous. As an example, I myself had seven scams attempted on me. I am sure it could have been worse. I know of a friend who had a few days with an individual, and when she got home, she found items missing from her suitcase. It can get a bit complicated for you if you decide to put private information out there about yourself, like your pictures and relationship information. This can be somewhat of a problem. I don't use the Internet much, but I have gotten into a little hot water by putting some friendly but personal information on Facebook. I had done this with good intentions, but some things have come back to bite me. My advice is to be careful about what you put out there.

A Few Changes

After I have called her a week or so in advance, I may arrive with a box of candy or flowers. I didn't start bringing flowers until I was older, in my twenties—and yes, I am old school. The last gal I dated, I would bring her flowers nearly every time we went out. We would go to the drive-in back in Iowa as well as California. The drive-in was very popular, or we would go skating, and our snack was popcorn and a soda. We may go to Lannie's Drive-In for a Special Lannie's sandwich, and then we would head home. And yes, I am sure Dad would drive her home, and most of the time I would call the date sometime the next day to see how she was doing or maybe ask for another date.

Now, let's look at today. First, dates do change, so the first date and the next ones can change. They also change with the couple's age. A date can take several forms. For the first date, you may be asked to pick a place where you feel good meeting someone, the time and location are given, and you drive your own cars there. You meet and talk, and depending on how interested she is in you, that will determine the time you spend with each other. When it comes to paying, I am from the old school, so I will offer to pay for the meal and drinks, but often in this case, the lady will offer to pay her own way. You might suggest for her to pick up the tip. There could be a few friends or a girlfriend along for the date. I have recommended that you do bring a girl along for safety purposes, but this is your decision. Today, you might go to a bar and watch sports; as you know, there are numerous TVs and different programs to see. I am not a drinking guy, so I might suggest a movie in the area, with a dinner before or after the film. This would be more like a second or third date. For me, the bar scene is not romantic, and it is very hard to communicate with your companion. I am hearing impaired, so this isn't a good place for me to have a romantic adventure. Often a second date might be at her home, where she would fix dinner, and there might be wine. You may watch a TV movie together. Of course I would bring flowers and maybe candy, but that's just me. I am not sure what your guy is going to do. I hope he does the right thing, but you will have to be the judge of that.

Let's talk about who pays. The rules about who picks up the bill have evolved, but I believe that in some quarters, until proven wrong, we older gentlemen still pick up the tab. But in the day, it was very much understood that if a guy asked a lady out on a day, he was going to foot the bill. Today this isn't so clear, and if one assumes that the guy is to pick up the bill, this could be conceived as being sexist, or you are some kind of chivalrous pig. Of course, this isn't everyone's opinion. Therefore, you should both agree ahead of time to make sure you are not debating the tab.

The Cell Phone

The cell phone is such a wonderful device, and at the same time it is a pain in the butt. We can pretty much assume that the person you are going to call tonight isn't waiting at home by the phone. Many homes today don't even have landlines these days. This device makes some communications easier, but that gal you are going to ask out can be out on a boat with another date, and when you call, she is sitting there with a margarita and him at her side. While you are talking to her on this highly impersonal device, she can check messages and can misunderstand your text. Cell phones can be a helpful tool, but at the same time they are a huge distraction.

Hooking up on the First Date Seems to Be More Common

The art of dating seems to be dying or is dead. Of course, I am kind of speaking out of both sides of my mouth, because I am going to assume that I am going to have two kinds of readers: some young women and also older women. Therefore, I am going to hope that there are still a few gentlemen out there. I was at a get-together yesterday, and I didn't know the guy, but he was telling me that he went dancing three times a week. I assumed that like me, he was more accustomed to dating—or courting, if you will. However, we are seeing this new culture where sex is accepted before the individuals really know each other, with sex on the first date. We have this group of individuals willing to hook up for this one-night relationship. They are not willing to put in the time to develop a relationship. In Dad's day, he may have had his eye on making it to first base, if you will, but more often than not he was more looking for the real prize: getting and keeping a gal as his wife, not just a one-night stand.

More than likely, today's singles are more interested in hooking up. They are not interested in putting in the time to develop a relationship.

But What Is the Cost of This Quickie Romance?

You can bet there is no free lunch in these one-night stands. Sexually transmitted diseases (STDs) are more prevalent than ever. For this quick encounter, the threat of an STD is much higher than in your parents' time. We are looking at more than three million cases being reported.

We find that the information today about the involvement and practice of safe sex is more prevent than during your parents (and my) time, however the risk is much greater.

I suggest you take my advice and avoid the one-night stand. Now, I am going to share a secret with you, and at the same time, I suggest that you might consider the same idea. A number of years ago, a gal and I got serious about one another, and though we really hadn't known one another for very long, we decided to have a closer relationship. We agreed to get tested for STDs, and the cost was free through the social welfare department. Neither one of us was infected. Take my advice, and I believe you will be much happier in the long run. If you are going to have an intimate relationship with an individual, get tested first.

So You Would Like to Date Younger Men

You meet this new guy at the local coffee house, and you both get this rush. He has this dry humor that kills you, and he has these bedroom eyes that turn you on. But you find that he was finishing his freshman year of high school at the same time you were receiving your BS from college.

Dating a man who is two or three years your junior can work, but being the older woman in a relationship can have its challenges. That said, the downside also comes with its perks. If you want this kind of thing to work, make sure you are up to the challenge.

When you enter a new relationship, you are going to bring the experience you had with the former gentlemen you have gone out with. But the new, younger man is likely going to have less baggage than you do. What you are going to discover is that men can have preconceived ideas about the women and their previous relationships that they bring to the table.

That said, fewer relationships mean less experience, but at the same time you should find him more open with you and your relationship.

At the same time, the less experience he has means it is very likely that he could lack relationship skills, like communication with you and resolving problems and conflicts. Therefore, you will need to choose your battles carefully and learn how to compromise on situations and things that are important to the relationship.

You can be confident that you are going to have dinner dates, but at the same time here come the five-mile hikes and bike rides on the weekend, and next come the movies, rock concerts, and other physical activities. There is no question that these guys can be as eventful in the bedroom as they are outside, and they will bring along this boyish youthfulness, bringing out your own youthful side.

You can expect him to treat you as smarter and worldlier, and he will want to please you not just physically but also intellectually and emotionally. You will find that he will search for creative dating ideas to bring romance and youth into your life, which will stimulate you and make you feel empowered and appreciated.

Often the men your age are taken, and this can be a very common reason why older women might seek younger men. There can be a lack of choice, but it can often return good results.

Older women can be in charge, and they feel that they can handle the twists and turns in the relationship because of their greater experience. A big advantage is in sex, because dating can get more difficult for women as they age. Older women can feel more confident because they bring more experience to the table. An older woman is going to have more experience in sex, which is better for both.

At the same time, younger men tend to be less serious. This can help by bringing less pressure to the table, and it can reduce any complications as you simply the company of the man.

Here is something I would like you to look at and really think about!

Are you willing to meet a nice guy who is fifty, seventy-five, or more than one hundred miles away from you? This is going to come up. I must share this. The distance thing came up more than once a week for me. I did talk to several, and I almost went for it with one or two. One was more than 150 miles away. In most cases, I didn't get further than the photo. Some were very nice looking, but a number of times during some of the conversations, it was said a number of the gals and could not move closer to me. I could more, but would and could are two different things.

If this comes up—and it will at some point—how much driving back and forth is it going to take for this relationship to work? Are you willing to do this? How often do you want to see him? You had better come up with this answer now. You can always change your mind. I would like to see my gal two or three times a week, maybe more. Fifty cents per mile in gas times fifty miles is twenty-five dollars one way.

Let's say he takes you out to dinner, and you pay for one dinner one a week. I took one gal out Friday night, and one out Sunday. They were about the same distances, but one was about $145 for the dinner, but including the fifty dollars for the driving costs, it was $195. The other was the Sunday date, for forty-five dollars, and I got her flowers, and the distance, so I paid $107. So unless he is a millionaire, you are going to have a little cash-flow issue here. That is I have set my range. Anyway, it's food for thought. But maybe you can pack a lunch for the both of you. I still don't think this is going to work well, but I could be wrong. It's going to take two very special people who make a strong connection to pull this off.

My girlfriend works all week, has a family, and like most of us has to go to the doctor, get her hair done, attend family activities, and more. The possibility of having weekends off or driving alone is not a good plan. I would not want her on the road late at night going back home, and I don't think she would either.

Now, I can remember driving for the Bay Area from south of San Francisco, to Rock Spring, Wyoming. This was quite a drive, but I was in my MG TD, and the radio was going. If it wasn't for the roar of the engine I would still be by the side of the road asleep. This was a lonely, dark drive, and I was about twenty-four. I don't think I could do this again and wouldn't want to try. No, at my age, I couldn't do it. And I have no idea what this costs now. Sure, I save the motel cost, but at what price?

You Don't Have to Be in the Dating Game to Realize That Something Has Changed the Game and the Rules

Yes, often the dating game is beyond recognition. Anyway, it was for me, and if you've been out here, I am sure it has for you too. With the Internet, we meet more people every day than ever before, but with the increase in choices come scams, players, and those who say, "I am not sure why I am here." Because of the increase in the number of candidates, I have found it more difficult to find a real, honest to goodness gal to go out with. How about you?

Of course, women are becoming more empowered, and men aren't sure how to connect with them in a way that is both attractive and respectful. If you are single now, it seems that it is time to take a new approach to love that is more up-to-date, modern, and suited for the times. Here are several ways that men should approach you for dating differently.

- **Look for men who attempt to pursue you and approach you by showing interest in you.**
  Over the years, men have been told that it's their job to go after women first or make the first move by asking them out, setting up the dates, and being the pursuer. This was considered their job. But this has been developing issues over time in building the right kind of relationships with the women. The men are focused on the chase, but they are not being choosy enough about whom they're chasing. Therefore, they are wasting their time on women who are not making an effort to make time

for them. Don't you gentlemen want someone who's interested in being with you and willing to make time for you? I assume the answer is yes! And ladies, this is where the point is brought home to you. You need to pick up these signals, because here is the same question: Don't you want to be with someone who cares for you too?

Men should be looking for women who aren't playing hard to get, and if they are, they need to stop. You guys need to stop tripping over yourself trying to win her; instead, you should be looking for women who respond quickly, write longer messages, and ask you questions. And those who don't repeatedly cancel dates. Gentlemen, choose women who know what they are looking for and who show genuine interest in you.

In my experience with dating sites, this has been one of my biggest criticisms. Many of the women that I have run into—this is more than four hundred—need to stop before they get involved. They should do some deep soul-searching to discover what they are looking for. If you are not sure of what you are looking for, then before you spend your hard-earned money, take some time to discover this for yourself. Otherwise you are wasting your time and money, and you are going to be frustrated and disappointed. These are some of the tools that you need to find your way back into a loving environment and situation.

- **Be more selective.**
  Yes, this is the advice you gals have gotten over and over, but this time it is for the guys. It is getting more important for you to be more selective about who you are dating. You guys should be listening to the message as well. Believe it or not, no woman wants to be asked out just because you think she is hot. What kind of message does this send? It is saying that you don't respect her as a person and don't hold up high standards for the people you spend time with. There are a lot of women and men out there, so you should have an idea of the types of qualities you want in the

person you are going to be dating. Having standards makes you more attractive and keeps you focused on who the person you are, not just how great he or she looks in a picture.

- **Maintain your own boundaries.**

  Here is an important message for both of you. You both have control over the rate or speed of your relationship. If either one of you feels that the rate of your relationship is going too fast (holy cow, did she just leave some of clothing in my hamper?), then slow down. You both have to respond for communication to work. Express your boundaries; this is one way to view your relationship, how you would like to be treated, and how you view the relationship. You will find that expressing yourself is one way to make it clear where you believe you are in the relationship. You may need to suggest that you have both been busy, but you really would like to spend more time getting to know each other.

The dating game has changed over the years, and men's and women's roles in the ritual aren't as clearly defined as they were. It's not just the guys who have something to learn.

Please don't assume your Prince Charming is going to be coming anytime soon. If you believe that the guy must make the first move, this may come as a shock, but some dating data is showing that women who make the first move are more successful at getting what they want. Are you ready? Data suggests if you gals send a message asking a guy to dinner, drinks, or lunch, you get about 75 percent more responses than the average woman. This seems to me a clear indicator that the guys are somewhat relieved to not have to send that first response to indicate that they are interested. If you are interested, don't always rely on the guys to make the first move. Be open and smart, and always give the guy the opportunity to connect with you. This is a smart choice, and it is going to increase your odds and opportunities. Both you and your date are equally responsible for controlling the pace of your relationship and determining whether you are moving too fast or slow.

Here is the thing: for more than fifty years, the roles in the ritual of dating have been pretty defined. This may or may not be a good thing, but with some of the changes that have come forward, it is now time for everyone to learn something.

- **Enjoy the moment you are in.**
  If you think that guys send mixed signals, don't be surprised, because it is a good chance that they don't recognize how things are going. If you don't recognize it, men generally approach dating in a more experimental way. I usually say that they are testing the waters or running it up the flagpole. They want to see how things are going. You will find that guys are very much relieved to find women who are direct communicators. So here's the advice: If you see an attractive guy profile, and it rocks your boat, take the step to send the first message. It can be as simple as a smile or saying hi. Yes, the smart approach is offering men the opportunity to connect with you. Don't rely solely on dating the guy who makes the first move on you.

  Also, give yourself time to connect with and explore how the guys you date fit into your life rather than going straight into the relationship scenario with them. Give yourself time to build some trust, a connection, and an understanding of what someone is about. All of this takes time. You need to slow down and enjoy getting to know people before you start planning your future.

- **Be clear about what you do and don't want.**
  If you find yourself in a situation that doesn't feel right, it may be better to fade into the darkness, gradually dropping out of contact with someone. If you are not interested in dating them, make it clear, but let them down in a way that is kind. Yes, it can be hard, but it is better in the long run. You can say, "Thank you, I had a great time meeting you the other evening. But I want to be

honest and up-front with you. I didn't feel the connection when we met, and I want to wish you well in your search." This can be a little challenging, but make the communication clear. Taking responsibility for our own actions and happiness is the right thing to do.

Let's Try This on for Size and See How It Fits!

Here are six ways to find the right partner for you.

1. If you were to go around the world, you would find that men and women have developed lists of attractions and top criteria for finding someone to marry. Some rank by personality traits. It has been determined by studies and research that the most successful and happiest couples are those who, regardless of what they think they want, end up with spouses who have excellent personality traits such as emotional stability and agreeability. These spouses have been clearly linked to marital and sexual satisfaction. Here is the thing: it is clear that it is better to be a warmer and more cooperative mate then an unstable and disagreeable one!

One may think that the spouses with these excellent traits sound boring. Most people want someone who is very attractive and interesting, and they think that they would be more willing to put up with someone who is moody and arrogant but also very attractive. This type of behavior gives the impression that their love and good moods must be earned. This action can put undue pressure on the other party, as well as unreasonable expectations.

2. Here are a few facts that you need to consider. The deal breaker can be more important in a relationship than reactions or a loving moment. It is like pouring ice water over the lovemaking phase of the relationship. There the two of you are, the lights are low, the lobster is great, and the music is wonderful. Then you recall that that the person told you he or she doesn't want children.

I would like you to make a list of the top five deal breakers. Don't take it lightly, and take your time.

Some Top Deal Breakers

1. Hates dogs
2. Doesn't like sex
3. Chews tobacco
4. Bathes two times a week or less
5. Doesn't want children
6. Hates cat
7. Uses drugs
8. Smokes
9. Reads or looks at sex magazines
10. Runs around the house in his/her underwear
11. Wears the other sex's clothes
12. Is unfaithful
13. Watches TV in bed
14. Dates other people
15. Gambles

16. Wants sex all the time
17. Does not take care of family members
18. Wants to have live-in parents
19. Is abusive
20. Doesn't share money
21. Dates both men and women
22. Thinks everything always must be in its place
23. Doesn't work
24. Does not help around the home

You might want to develop your own list of deal breakers.

As an example, I have a friend who has hairless jungle lizards, and some people keep snakes. Some drink too much, are always in debt and financial trouble, or gamble. I really don't like snakes because I don't like things that don't have hair.

Once the honeymoon is over, that is when the arguments start and the romance disappears. You will find the most common things that people too often have to deal with are smoking, financial issues, drinking, and drugs. Those traits relate to major lifestyle choices.

Other deal breakers could seem futile to some, such as hair color or taste in films. Yes, it is true that deal breakers are unique to every individual, and you should be honest, even if one appears to be superficial. Once the shine wears off the pot, don't think, "I can get used to that over time." That never happens—the deal breaker becomes a larger pain in the side over time.

Often different people have various relationships, and as relationships grow and blossom over time, they often realize what they once deemed a must-have doesn't matter so much, and they learn to compromise. But if some of these traits emerge over time and become highly problematic, such as bad temper, flirtatiousness, alcohol abuse, major problems with sexual appetites, and so forth, it can be better to move on from that relationship.

Recently, I was talking with a longtime friend, and I told him that I was trying to write a couple of books on dating. He said, "Interesting. I am kind of going through a dilemma myself. What area are you working in?" I told him it was a deal breaker. He replied, "Hey, I believe I have a couple." What were they? "Well, I met Judy about nine months ago, and as you know, you start talking about this and that. We got to, What church did you go to when you were younger, and now? I told her that I was a Methodist, but I don't go to church regularly, and of course she tells me that she is a Baptist, but that doesn't make a lot of difference because she doesn't attend regularly either. But that was then, and now we are talking about getting married, and she is suggesting there may be a problem. Could be a deal breaker, right?" I told him no question. This should have been worked out before. He told me, "I thought we had." This is true!

Here is my advice for both of you: don't take lightly what people believe/ Often the conviction goes much deeper than you (or they) might think.

A very long time ago, I dated a nice Catholic girl who was twenty-three years old. First, she was an only child, so this should have been a red flag from the get-go. Not only was she very close to her parents, but she was a "good Catholic girl." She also got drunk a lot, and I kind of overlooked this; I myself am not much of a drinker. How many deal breakers do you see here? I can assure you that after a time, our marriage would have been in trouble. As it was, I did do the Catholic pre marriage class that was required. I don't believe I would have become a Catholic at that time. Her parents got her to call off the wedding twice. I took my rings back and moved along. Some of the things you might adjust to over time, but that may not always be true. It would be better to move along early, before you fall in love, because that can result in broken hearts and arguments. The older you get, it may be even more important because old people don't have as much time as younger people do. It doesn't make it any easier, however. It is best to clear up this issue before it becomes a problem.

At this point, with the first gal I was going to marry, I believe that had I not walked away, the deal breakers would have caused a great deal of trouble. A year or two later, I did cross this bridge, and I was exposed to what again could very likely be a deal breaker with the second woman. I did take a chance with what could have been a deal breaker, and we were married for thirty years and happy for about twenty-eight. Not once did it come up. She wanted me to join the Latter-Day Saints' church, and I got baptized and never looked back. I am asking you to take every one of these possible deal breakers seriously, because there is more than one person who can be deeply affected: your potential spouse, you, the parents, any children, and more. This is not just a little bump in the highway of life—this could be a major pothole. Please remember no one is perfect, but you should prioritize your deal breakers and be careful. Please don't compromise much, though it is okay to be flexible when you can.

The following is a "real" story. The gentlemen in this story, Ernie, had been dating Rose for some time now. Yes, they were close, but he lived some distance away from Rose—in fact, three hundred miles away. This in itself could be a deal breaker, but in this case we are not going to discuss what could be an issue. On his last visit, he stopped by my place and told his story. First, Rose has a son in his late twenties, fathered by another gentleman, but he wasn't married to Rose or providing any support for this child. We can deal with these other issues at another time.

The nine dogs of various sizes are welcome into the bedroom, and bed, by Rose. Ernie suggested to me that he wasn't comfortable with this arrangement. Even the dogs were not happy with the arrangement.

There are several issues here. The dogs could do their personal business someplace in the house. Are you willing to allow these animals to run carefree throughout this home, and to sleep on the bed with you and your partner, or are you going to draw the line somewhere? At my home, that is a major deal breaker. Yes, my fiancée and I had a discussion over a similar situation. I have two dogs, not nine, and my dogs are trained to go outside to handle any personal business. My fiancée said to me that we must have a partition at the door of our room to not allow the dogs into this part of our home, and we agreed on this. But we had a discussion and agreement on this subject—twice.

What we see here is that Ernie may allow the dogs in the bedroom until the shine wears off the apple, and then she explodes at the situation. This can be a deal breaker, but it should be resolved before they consider marriage.

I have a few friends who know I am trying to make a help book on dating using the Internet, but by now I am hoping it is really more than that. Anyway, I got a call from a friend, and he told me that the part on deal breakers was correct. Let's call him Frank.

He told me that he had shared some of my ideas with his girlfriend; we will call her Shelly. Frank was talking about the deal breakers. Frank said that Shelly doesn't want to give up some of the things she wants to do and when she wants to do them. Frank told her he would like to go out with a couple of his friends to have a beer with them, but she told him that he could not go. He said to her, "But you are not willing to give up doing the various things you want to do. Why can't I do some of the things I want to do?"

Her answer was simply, "Because."

Some deal breakers have to be worked out. You can go along with them now while there is the love in the air, but after a few months or years, there is a good chance you will become unhappy. This kind of thing will create a lot of problems in your marriage. I told Frank he needed to take care of this and agree on the things that they could do and be happy with.

Remember, it is not always other women, smoking, not showering, or drinking too much. That little thing he or she does can become a big thing. I have a friend who has a gal, and from time to time, he likes to give her a pat on the head. She gets mad at him and says to him, "I am not a dog." He tells me that to him, it is a sign of endearment to him.

Don't Be Impressed by the Veneer

What is glittering may be fool's gold. I hate to say this, but there are a lot of women who sell themselves short and are going for men with shiny exteriors. You will find that a guy who is more concerned with his material things has no more room to value anyone else—including you. This kind of attitude is confusing to me. Just because a guy is (or thinks he is) good looking, wears a cool suit, drives a new car, and has a pricey watch, it doesn't mean this is a great guy. It may be just the opposite. You might find out later that his mom is paying the rent. Hey, what is wrong with the guy in jeans or driving last year's F-150? You may be tripping over dollars to pick up pennies. That Rolex may not be checking the time. See if he is overdrawn at the bank. Here is the point: never be impressed by a man's overvalued assets (boat, clothes, homes, apartment, or wheels) in the first place. It might be his family's money, or he owes the bank a lot. If you want to be impressed with what he has, be smart enough to check his net worth.

Another thing: Keep a close eye on the guy who is throwing around money. This boyfriend booked an upscale hotel room and filled it with cut roses and a couple of pricey gifts. She was so surprised that he went all-out for her. On one hand, you have to give the guy kudos for his performance. But he had to pay a ton for these flashy gifts to get to that glowing smile. No, he didn't go too far out of the way, because he was living at home with his mom and dad. But the gal could not see beyond the image to reality. It may have been a nice thing to do and a flattering gesture, but if he is living with his parents, he more than likely has little to no funds. This is more than likely a foolish gesture, and you really can't reward someone for being reckless and spending other people's money.

The key is applauding your man whenever he exercises good and prudent judgment. Don't reward him for being dumb and using poor judgment. If he has the funds, this is something else. But there is a red flag here when poor judgment is used.

Whatever you do, please don't ignore the red flags. Often women will turn a blind eye to these red flags and warning signs, even though they are hitting them right in the face.

Red Flags

Lives with his parents
Drives an expense car, but it is rented
Overaccessorizes
Has more than one ring on one hand, more than one bracelet per wrist, or more than one necklace
Overdresses
Spends money regardless of price
Approaches you with flattering but rehearsed lines
Suggests that he has a job but can't tell you what he does
Doesn't talk much about you, only himself
Asks you to hold money or to pay while you are on a date

Here Are Some Tips on Dating for You by Guys!

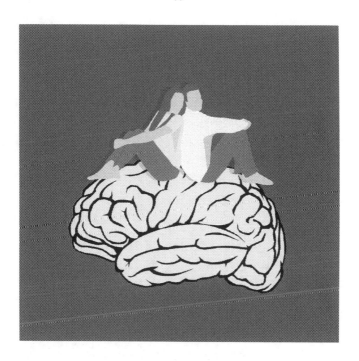

It is your choice to take them, try them and see how they work for you. I am sure that you may have heard this advice before, so it may sound familiar to you? Yes, for a lack of something else to call it, Dating is difficult for us to play, important, but at the same time very challenging.

1. **It's always best to be yourself**
   I am sure this ring in your ear, it is better off in a dating scenario, that one be themselves. Don't try to be someone you are not, just be relaxed and let the date be just you and your new acquaintances. Really you will be much better, because it causes a lot fewer problems and issues down the road.

2. **Go in with reasonable expectations and an open mind**
   One of the biggest issues from the beginning of time is the problem of people not listening to one another and keeping an open mind.

And the dating world is on exception. If you really listen to your date asking you questions and showing that you are interested in what he has to say, one you will show him that you are interested, and at the same time have a better chance that he / they will do the same thing for you. And it provides you with another benefit, which is letting you know that there is a chance that you are compatible quicker.

3. **And remember the most important, thing here is to have fun**
First leave all your experience at the door. Always relax and enjoy the evening. Order whatever you want, laugh, listen, and just have a normal conversation like you would anyplace. Again, be yourself, and talk about normal stuff, don't try to make stuff up.

So, see if these tips will make it easier for you in your dating situations….

Yes, I would like to talk to you about your profile, not this along with how you look is going to really start to open the door for you and for that matter, when you are viewing his profile it does the same thing. Now think about it. As an example, if you were evaluating a nice-looking guy, and this is assuming he did what I have been suggesting, have a nice, if one can, a professional or near professional photo. This guy or woman may be your next boyfriend or for that matter husband, girlfriend, or wife, are you thinking in these terms? And why not, is this a game to you? You don't have to answer that for me, but you. First, you have put up good money to participate, time, and energy. I don't know about you, but I want to be as successful as I can in the shortest amount of time. I don't have the same amount of time as I did 50 years ago.

I am going to share this with you. I have been on about four of these sites, with one thing in mind, I wanted really, to find me a nice gal, and yes this might sound hokey, and we both ride off together into the sun set, isn't this what you want? Now again, you are answering this question for you, if you haven't asked yourself why you are on the sites, you need to. I have gone out with, a few women that, said to me, one I don't have time to date, I have a lot of thing going on, or I have to babysit for my daughter, is this is the case, why waste your time, or mine for that matter, if you really not interested in meeting an one? Not to say that everyone you meet you want or would go out with that you meet. But to make the determination, before you meet anyone is, a little counter production don't you think?

In one way or another, I talked to more than 400 women, some of the communications, got a little warm, and interesting, some gals were flat not interested, some were, some were too far away, some cold, but I was out there for nearly 2-/1/2 years, is this what you want. I have gotten discouraged at times. Yes, have you too? So, let's move on…..

First, and I have said this, have the best photo you have, whatever it takes let us look as good as we can. Do I mean going to the beauty shop? Yes, I mean take the time to make yourself look as great as you can down to your socks! You are going to feel better, and look better, and have more confidence. Now think about this for a moment, if you were going to put your car up for sale, wouldn't you try to clean it up, maybe new tires, run it through the car wash and so on?

Now, I would like to suggest that, if you say that you like to fish, if you are looking for an outdoor type of a guy, first make sure you know how, how to talk the talk, and walk the walk. Yes, you might have you in a photo fishing, batting hook, but do not do this, or say this, if it isn't out and out a fact. Now for me, I am not in pressed, I want to get my fish cook and from a restaurant, in fact myself and a nice looking 5-5" gal and I were out recently, for a fish dinner for my birthday, and I don't care one bit that she didn't cook it, but I was more impressed that she got me to and from the restaurant. We were in Dallas and I don't know my way around, and at night, it gets even worse.

Now, I kind of believe that yes, to target the kind of guy that you are looking for, so you are not disappointed, but at the same time, you need to tell the truth, if you don't know how to sail, don't suggest that you do. Lately, I go to the range about 2 times a week, I am down somewhat, but yes, I don't kind of collect and fire most of my weapons, I fire for sport and I hunt wild pigs a few times a year. So yes, if you suggested that you were involved in shooting, I would be interested, and to tell the truth, the young lady I was out with the other night suggest that she was interested, I was excited to meet her, and maybe I shouldn't say this, we are dating, and I got her a handgun as a special gift, and we are also shooting together, as well as other actives, things that she likes to do too.

I don't believe that men and women must be both into everything, together and she golfs, the last time I was at a golf course was when I was 15 and tried to work as a caddy. In fact, as we got better acquainted, how I felt about her going out with her buddies to play golf, I said fine, I can do some of the things I like to do. You don't over time, want to be with him every minute of your life nor do I. He is going to want some time with the boys as you will with your friends, but you can over do this too. As it has been said everything in moderation.

Focus on the real things are for or against, I did have one gal I believe she was in Austin, and this really doesn't matter, however it is another issue to look at, but she tells me up front that if I am not a Democrat don't get In Touch. So, if you are a dyed in the wool Republican, let us know, and if you really don't like guys that chew, smoke, shave, or whatever you are for or against, this is where you do your selling, but tell the truth. I myself, I hate to say this, and it may come my childhood, but If you are overweight, or under let us know, my mother, was a tall 6' lady, and overweight, not saying this is bad, because there is someone for everyone, but it is kind of nice to get off on the right foot.

If you like to swim, but never have, let us know. Now I would like to scuba Dive, I am not a good swimmer, but I am willing to learn. There is this approach too. I used to own a horse and ride and I was talking to my new girlfriend, and was talking about taking her riding, and she said, she doesn't like to do this anymore. So, there are a lot of ways you can play this. Another example, I was driving along, and I looked to my left, and there is this indoor skydiving, well I have never done this, nor I am not interested, but you might be able to turn this into an interesting date. I just might give this a try, if you were so inclined.

So in conclusion, paint your profile as clear as you can with truths, and in describing what you are interested in and what you are looking for and willing to do, also make this clear too.

And, make the product sound as good, and look as good as you can. Do I sound like an old salesman, well good, because I was, I used to work for P & G. And anyone from P & G, or most salespeople will agree with me, you want to make your product as appealing as you can. And in this case, it will be a win-win for you, because you are the product and you are the one that is going to benefit.

What should Boyfriends and Girlfriends Be Talking about During Private Time?

- Listen. You might hear your partner talking about which movie to go to. You might find them on the couch discussing two or three, or other things they like. You might discuss specific films and whether or not you enjoy them. I know my gal and I have a little contest, and when she picks a winner, she gets the next pick. If I pick a winner, I get the next pick.
- We also discussed where we should go for dinner. This decision can get a little heated, because she is a vegetarian and I am the cow eater. But I try to let her win most of the time.
- How are your jobs going?
- In our case, we are a little older, so what is going on at the doctor visits?
- Some might talk about how to cook, with one teaching the other.
- We have talked about getting a new house.
- The truth is most of all of us, no matter what age, are talking about the same things, but younger folks may talk a little more about sex.
- Some politics.
- The economy.
- The price of gas.
- How we want to fix up our home.
- How we dress.
- Family.

What You Will Find Here Are Things to Help a Woman Find a Great Husband

Here is the thing everyone wants to know they're loved and you can be assured that wives rarely tire of hearing those three little words—"I love you"—from their husbands and I am sure you enjoy hearing them too. . However, showing your spouse how you feel can be equally important as telling her—it may be a cliché, but actions really can speak louder than words. One of the things I try to do is almost every time I see my gal, I take her flowers. In fact, the best ways to express how you feel are usually in simple, seemingly unimportant acts like giving her an unexpected hug or holding hands when you walk together. I make a point of holding her hand every chance I get. And I am not a young guy, and to tell you the truth, I enjoy it too..

Understanding and Forgiveness

There will be days when your wife will make mistakes or when she'll be difficult to be around. No one (and that includes you too) is perfect. She both wants and deserves your willingness to understand and forgive her. Remember that no relationship, and especially marriage, can be sustained without forgiveness. I remember, the time before I lost my wife Bobbie, she was having trouble driving her car, and almost caused a major auto accident that would or just injured the two of us. Not only was I somewhat upset, and a little scared too, but I realized she was really trying, so I just left this issue alone, and we went on with our getting to the restaurant.

Women especially want you to understand that the hormonal fluctuations that impact her mood are very real. So don't make fun of her or say she's "crazy" when she's got her period or is pregnant or going through menopause. Be empathic and understanding instead, this was also true, with the issue that my wife was having with some problem associated with

110

her cancer, I was just trying to help her anyway I could dealing with these issues.

Real Conversation

Don't let your conversations with your wife dwindle to nothing but talk about your kids, your jobs, and the weather. If that happens, it could be a sign that your marriage is in real trouble. There's lots more to talk about beyond the practical and the superficial. In fact, it's critical for couples to <u>discuss their feelings and emotions</u> on a regular basis. These deep and real conversations are the "glue" that will hold you together and create the intimacy married people desire. I must share with you that in the last days before I lost my wife to cancer, we stopped talking about real issues and problems, and really started to drift even further apart, avoiding the real issues, which overtook us.

Quality Time with Her (and Your Children)

Having quality time with your wife and kids isn't something that just happens. You have to make these moments of connection happen by both arranging for them and then following through. Spending time with those you love must be a high priority for you. This is so true, I have lost both my kids, and grandkids, somehow, I managed to miss the boat, I have all but lost my entire family.

It's also important to remember that the woman you married is your wife, not just the mother of your children. Never stop trying to romance and date her. After all, that's how the two of you grew close in the first place. Common activities lead to shared feelings and help strengthen your bond. Looking back we, I believe, had this great relationship, but we allow to let Cancer and other physical factors to get between us. I am going to try to suggest trying to not let this happen, will it take a lot of work? You bet!.

To Hear "Yes" More Than "No"

Whether it's having her decorating ideas dismissed or hearing the dreaded "not tonight," no wife likes being turned down. Occasional rejections are one thing though; <u>habitual negative responses</u> to her and your kids are another story—and not one that often ends well. Constantly hearing "no" can wear them down and cause resentment that pushes them away from you. Looking back, I can tell you now, giving up a few ball games, or programs on TV that you like is a lot easier, that to wake up in the middle of the night and not finding her by your side was and is extremely hard to understand and deal with. And also knowing that she is never coming back can tear at your heart every day.

That's not to say you should become a pushover and just say yes. But try thinking twice before automatically saying "no" and you might be pleasantly surprised at how it can improve your relationships. Research shows that the more you respond to requests in a positive way, the happier and more satisfying your relationship will be. I spent over 6 and a half years alone, and the lack of sound was dealing. We talked less, and less, and then she couldn't, and she was gone.

Better Listening Skills

It's really disheartening for a wife to share her thoughts and <u>feelings</u> with her mate and then realize he didn't actually listen to her. Your wife wants you to not only listen with your ears but to listen with your heart. Besides hearing the words she speaks, it's important to be open to what your partner has to say, even if you don't agree with it. <u>According to research,</u> men who respect their wives' opinions have much happier marriages. And, guess what: Often their wives will be right! Try to believe and follow the concept, but I am sure, I failed the "Happy life, Happy wife", but I did lose her to cancer.

Affection and Kindness

How often do you say "please" or "thank you" or give your spouse an unexpected kiss? Unfortunately, some married couples forget that being kind to and affectionate with one another are keys to a successful marriage—they help feed the relationship and keep it strong. Think about when you were boyfriend and girlfriend: These were behaviors you probably did regularly and spontaneously. There's no reason they should stop when you're married. In fact, they may be even more important once you tie the knot, since research shows that the frequency with which you and your partner express and receive affection is directly related to your commitment and satisfaction.

Shared Household and Child-Rearing Responsibilities

One of the main reasons couples fight is conflict over who's doing what around the house. Chores and child care are not the sole responsibility of your wife. She shouldn't have to ask you to do your share around the house. You will be a hero in her eyes if you readily help when asked or—even better—take care of some chores before she asks. Bonus: You may benefit in the bedroom, too, since studies show women feel more sexually attracted to partners who pitch in. Try to be on top of some of the things that she does for you and the kids, not I didn't have the child issue some much because the kids were going by the time we were getting together, on the other hand I did have kids with my first wife, so I am sure, I could have done a better job.

A Day Off Now and Then

Don't fuss about your wife taking a day off a couple of times a month. This means she'll be free from worrying about what's happening with the kids, the house, the pets, and you. She deserves this break in her schedule and she needs to provide it for herself in order to be emotionally and physically healthy. Help her to have a fun day once and awhile, plan a surprise once and a while for and with her. One thing I do now, I take my fiance to get our nails done, or a massage. She will enjoy this, and you will too!

A Healthier Attitude About Their Health

It's not a stereotype that men are terrible at taking care of themselves when it comes to their health: <u>Research shows</u> it's true. And all that "persuasion" your wife must use to get you to go to the doctor or dentist isn't fair to her—she's your lover, not your mother. Part of the reason men don't prioritize healthcare is due to an ingrained idea about masculinity and strength: They feel pressure to appear strong and equate illness or pain with weakness. A better philosophy is that caring for yourself is the path to caring for your family.

Was this page helpful?

In my opinion, I am going to suggest that all too often, in the beginning of a relationship, many of us are willing to let our deal breakers slip by in the name of "love." I suggest that if you truly see a deal breaker that troubles you, know that the little bump in the road is going to become a massive pothole. You had better solve it now or else move on. I am not trying to break up your loving relationship. I am simply pointing out what can happen over time.

What Should Be Going on or Be Talked about in a Happy Relationship?

Now here are several good topics to talk about in a relationship

- You can nearly always use these conversation ideas that can be repeated in your time together, and the best part about these topics is that you're going to find that your partner will nearly always have a new answer each time you ask most of these questions.

- You can use these questions with your boyfriend or girlfriend or use them even if you are married.

- Using these topics, you'll realize just how easily you can build the chemistry and love in your relationship, just by talking about the right subjects.

- **Planning for the weekend.** Talk about your weekend plans together even if it's still early in the week. And can be exciting and fun, and it'll give both of you something to look forward to after a long week of work.

- By having something to look forward to, it'll even help both of you get through the week with enthusiasm because you know you have a good weekend coming up.

- **2 Compliments.** Talk about the things you like or admire about your partner. Let them know just how much you appreciate them, be it about their personality or about something they did the earlier week. [Read: 25 compliments for guys they'll never forget]

- **Daily worries.** 'So, what's been worrying you lately?' sounds so simple, but yet, it's something that can make your partner feel grateful and cared for. Even if they have no worries, just knowing that you care would make them feel good about being in the relationship.

- **4 Work.** There's always something to talk about work, be it a new project or a bad boss. By talking about each other's work life, it'll help both of you understand each other's professional sides and ethics better.

- **5 The little secrets.** Secrets are always fun to talk about. You can talk about secrets as a game where each of you have to take turns to reveal one new secret. It'll be a lot of fun, and both of you can get to know each other more intimately.

- **6 Movies and TV shows.** There's always something new and fun every week when it comes to movies and shows. Talk about each other's favorite shows or the movies both of you are excited to watch. [Read: 25 signs he loves you even if he doesn't say it out loud]

- **7 Food and restaurants.** Even if your lover isn't passionate about cooking, they'd at least appreciate good food. Talk about new restaurants or places both of you should visit over the weekend or on a special day. It'll give both of you a chance to explore cuisines together and also make dinner plans for the weeks to come.

- **8 Personal dreams.** Talk about your dreams with your partner. Tell them what you intend to do or what your visions and dreams are. It'll make for great conversations, and help your partner get to know your personal side better.
- **9 Vacations.** Plan your vacations or weekend getaways weeks or even months earlier. Vacations are almost always the highlight of an entire calendar year, so even dreamily planning it ahead of time can get both of you excited.
- **10 Hobbies and personal interests.** What do you enjoy doing in your own private time? Share your thoughts with your lover. Chances are, your partner too may have a few hobbies that you like.
- **11 Friends.** It's always good to know more about each other's friends. It's a step closer to learning more about your partner's life and what they do, especially when you aren't around. [Read: 13 signs your friends are ruining your perfect relationship]
- **12 Proud moments.** Ask your boyfriend or girlfriend to tell you about the moments in life when they've felt really proud of their own achievements. Memorable moments and childhood memories always provide for hours of fun, hilarious conversations.
- **13 Offer help.** Ask your partner if you could help them with something, even if it's as silly as a chore. Working together on tasks always brings two people closer. And it'll always make your partner feel grateful for having you around.
- **14 Five year plans.** If you've been dating for a while, talk about where you see yourself five years from now as a couple. Having shared goals always makes the relationship stronger and gives both of you something to work towards.
- **15 Self improvement.** When you talk about your own flaws and where you'd like to improve, it helps your partner feel more relaxed and comfortable, and they'd break down their own high walls and talk about their vulnerabilities too.

- **16 Families.** Talking about each other's families gives hours of interesting details and gossip. And it also helps make first introductions and spending time with family more fun. [Read: Things to know before you meet your partner's parents for the first time]

- **17 Problems in the bedroom.** Never push problems in the bedroom under the carpet. At some point, they'll always come back to haunt both of you. If you aren't able to perform or don't feel like having sex all of a sudden, talk about it so both of you can overcome any issues together.

- **18 Sex talk.** For a relationship to be successful, sexual intimacy is as important as romantic gestures. Talk about your sexually sensitive spots and erogenous zones, positions you like or want to try, your secret sexual fantasies and whatever it is that turns you on in bed. It'll be exciting and revealing at the same time. [Read: How to spice up your sex life in 30 sexy ways]

- **19 Wellbeing and wellness.** While health issues may not be easy to talk about, it's still a great way to get to know each other and enhance each other's lives.

- **20 Advice.** Communication isn't always about getting to know more about each other. Every now and then, offer advice and share your suggestions on what your lover could do to improve their life or their work.

- **21 Your past.** The past is always exciting and fun to talk about. You don't need to talk about past relationships or your sexual details if that makes you feel uncomfortable. But talk about your childhood, your young dreams and all the little things that make you who you are. [Read: The right way to talk about your past relationships]

- **22 The future.** What do you want to do with your life? This topic can make for intellectual conversations that can help you get to know your partner's view about life and the pursuits that matter to them.

- **23 Preferences.** Sometimes, it's the little things that can give both of you hours of fun conversations. Talk about each other's likes and dislikes. After all, preferences always change with time, and the more you know about your partner's present preference, the better you'd know them. [Read: <u>13 interesting things to talk about with your girlfriend</u>]

- **24 Shared goals.** Plan shared goals together. It could be about painting a wall, running a marathon the next year or just about anything else. When you plan things or try something new together, it brings both of you closer. [Read: <u>10 perfect things to talk about with your boyfriend</u>]

- **25 Personal opinions.** If you truly love each other, don't hold your thoughts back if you want to share what's on your mind with your lover. It doesn't matter if it's a suggestion or a warning, if you feel it, say it. Your partner will feel good to know that you're always looking out for them no matter what. It always feels good, doesn't it, when you know that you have a special someone who cares so much about you?

- [Read: <u>The 10 types of love you'll definitely experience in your lifetime</u>]

- **Use these topics to talk about in your relationship, and you'll never run out of interesting conversations. And both of you will feel closer to each other with each passing day too.**

Use these 25 topics, and you'll realize just how easily you can build the chemistry and love in your relationship, just by talking about the right things. [Read: <u>How to create sexual chemistry and make it stay</u>]

- **1 Plans for the weekend.** Talk about your weekend plans together even if it's still Monday evening. It's exciting and fun, and it'll give both of you something to look forward to after a long week of work.

By having something to look forward to, it'll even help both of you get through the week with enthusiasm because you know you have a good weekend coming up.

- **2 Compliments.** Talk about the things you like or admire about your partner. Let them know just how much you appreciate them, be it about their personality or about something they did the earlier week. [Read: 25 compliments for guys they'll never forget]

- **3 Daily worries.** So, what's been worrying you lately?' sounds so simple, but yet, it's something that can make your partner feel grateful and cared for. Even if they have no worries, just knowing that you care would make them feel good about being in the relationship.

- **4 Work.** There's always something to talk about work, be it a new project or a bad boss. By talking about each other's work life, it'll help both of you understand each other's professional sides and ethics better.

- **5 The little secrets.** Secrets are always fun to talk about. You can talk about secrets as a game where each of you have to take turns to reveal one new secret. It'll be a lot of fun, and both of you can get to know each other more intimately.

- **6 Movies and TV shows.** There's always something new and fun every week when it comes to movies and shows. Talk about each other's favorite shows or the movies both of you are excited to watch. [Read: 25 signs he loves you even if he doesn't say it out loud]

- **7 Food and restaurants.** Even if your lover isn't passionate about cooking, they'd at least appreciate good food. Talk about new restaurants or places both of you should visit over the weekend or on a special day. It'll give both of you a chance to explore cuisines together and also make dinner plans for the weeks to come.

- **8 Personal dreams.** Talk about your dreams with your partner. Tell them what you intend to do or what your visions and dreams are. It'll make for great conversations, and help your partner get to know your personal side better.

- **9 Vacations.** Plan your vacations or weekend getaways weeks or even months earlier. Vacations are almost always the highlight of an entire calendar year, so even dreamily planning it ahead of time can get both of you excited.

- **10 Hobbies and personal interests.** What do you enjoy doing in your own private time? Share your thoughts with your lover.

Chances are, your partner too may have a few hobbies that you like.

- **11 Friends.** It's always good to know more about each other's friends. It's a step closer to learning more about your partner's life and what they do, especially when you aren't around. [Read: 13 signs your friends are ruining your perfect relationship]

- **12 Proud moments.** Ask your boyfriend or girlfriend to tell you about the moments in life when they've felt really proud of their own achievements. Memorable moments and childhood memories always provide for hours of fun, hilarious conversations.

- **13 Offer help.** Ask your partner if you could help them with something, even if it's as silly as a chore. Working together on tasks always brings two people closer. And it'll always make your partner feel grateful for having you around.

- **14 Five year plans.** If you've been dating for a while, talk about where you see yourself five years from now as a couple. Having shared goals always makes the relationship stronger and gives both of you something to work towards.

- **15 Self improvement.** When you talk about your own flaws and where you'd like to improve, it helps your partner feel more relaxed and comfortable, and they'd break down their own high walls and talk about their vulnerabilities too.**16 Families.** Talking about each other's families gives hours of interesting details and gossip. And it also helps make first introductions and spending time with family more fun. [Read: Things to know before you meet your partner's parents for the first time]

- **17 Problems in the bedroom.** Never push problems in the bedroom under the carpet. At some point, they'll always come back to haunt both of you. If you aren't able to perform or don't feel like having sex all of a sudden, talk about it so both of you can overcome any issues together.

- **18 Sex talk.** For a relationship to be successful, sexual intimacy is as important as romantic gestures. Talk about your sexually sensitive spots and erogenous zones, positions you like or want to try, your secret sexual fantasies and whatever it is that turns you on in bed. It'll be exciting and revealing at the same time. [Read: How to spice up your sex life in 30 sexy ways]

- **19 Wellbeing and wellness.** While health issues may not be easy to talk about, it's still a great way to get to know each other and enhance each other's lives.
- **20 Advice.** Communication isn't always about getting to know more about each other. Every now and then, offer advice and share your suggestions on what your lover could do to improve their life or their work.
- **21 Your past.** The past is always exciting and fun to talk about. You don't need to talk about past relationships or your sexual details if that makes you feel uncomfortable. But talk about your childhood, your young dreams and all the little things that make you who you are. [Read: The right way to talk about your past relationships]
- **22 The future.** What do you want to do with your life? This topic can make for intellectual conversations that can help you get to know your partner's view about life and the pursuits that matter to them.
- **23 Preferences.** Sometimes, it's the little things that can give both of you hours of fun conversations. Talk about each other's likes and dislikes. After all, preferences always change with time, and the more you know about your partner's present preference, the better you'd know them. [Read: 13 interesting things to talk about with your girlfriend]
- **24 Shared goals.** Plan shared goals together. It could be about painting a wall, running a marathon the next year or just about anything else. When you plan things or try something new together, it brings both of you closer. [Read: 10 perfect things to talk about with your boyfriend]
- **25 Personal opinions.** If you truly love each other, don't hold your thoughts back if you want to share what's on your mind with your lover. It doesn't matter if it's a suggestion or a warning, if you feel it, say it. Your partner will feel good to know that you're always looking out for them no matter what. It always feels good,

doesn't it, when you know that you have a special someone who cares so much about you?

- No matter how long you've been in a relationship, it's always communication that brings two lovers closer together, and leads to better understanding.

Things to Not Discuss

1. BEING YELLED AT FOR BEING EMOTIONAL

There are a few exceptions; however, girls tend to be the more emotional of the genders. This is just the way women work. So, guys need to let women release their emotional side and not judge for it.

The absolute worst thing a man can do during an emotional situation is to start preaching about being emotional. It's your right.

2. DISCUSSING HOW MUCH MONEY YOU REALLY HAVE

Money is stressful for most people. When it comes to relationships it's often a deal breaker. If a man happens to makes more money than his women does, she definitely doesn't need to be bitch about how much money her have and make her feel bad. When it comes to discussing finances, just keep it simple.

Your women don't need to know what you make, and you don't need to pressure her in any way about money. That's a smooth move.

3. RELATING HER ACTIONS TO HER HORMONES

Men should not get involved in asking or suggesting anything about this, you are right to give him trouble for it.

You should never be related to emotions to the time of the month. That's so freakin' lame.

You have no idea because the woman's hormonal cycle does what it wants. You are best to refrain from any comments here.

4. DON'T ASK HER ABOUT HER SEXUAL PAST

A man should never be asked about a women's your pass sexual history, he is going to think about this, but he needs to think clearly before he asked the question. In other words, he needs to be prepared for the answer. A few years back, I was dating this woman, and she started to tell me some of her history. I stopped her and told her, I didn't want to know, and for a long-time, what she told me troubled me. You are better off not knowing, as she is better off not knowing yours.

We all have a sexual past. Tell me how that helps in the future, I don't think it does, or will.

For sure, if you love this girl, this question will make you angry; that's natural. Just don't ask, please.

5. COMMENTING ON HER MAKEUP-FREE FACE

There's no question that the first few dates are always going to bring out the best in you. Men need to understand you can't expect a woman to be perfect all the time.

You are going to show up looking like crap sometimes. That's okay.

They need to accept this is a perfect part of your relationship.

6. ASKING FOR COUPLE ACTIVITIES THAT YOU AREN'T GOING TO BE INVOLVED WITH

If you are going to suggest things like dieting or exercising solo, you're on the wrong track. However, if you can discuss these issues together, that's a smart move.

7. ASKING HER ABOUT HOW SHE LIKES TO SELF-INDULGE

It's important that you don't push her here. Understanding her pleasures is important but pushing her too far isn't a good thing. Open the door to conversation, but don't make her feel embarrassed.

8.   DISCUSSING YOUR UNION

So many men have screwed themselves by talking about the mistakes of the past.

They open the door to the past and start talking about the women they shouldn't have dated. Do yourself a favor and leave the past where it belongs, in the past.

Of course, you need to talk about what you screwed up on, but you also need to talk about what might work.

9.   TRASH-TALKING HER HAIRSTYLE OR CLOTHES

There's no doubt what a gal is wearing means everything. It really doesn't matter how beautiful your gal is…if you are dissing her hairstyle or what she is wearing, you are screwed.

It's important she understands what you are thinking and feeling. However, you need to tell her the truth.

10. TRYING TO COMPARE HER WILL DRIVE HER NUTS

We all try to compare ourselves to other people.

You are barking up the wrong tree if you start comparing your girlfriend to any other woman. Chances are your girlfriend has some insecurities and she's likely sensitive about her looks. When you start talking about how beautiful other women are, you could be making your girlfriend feel jealous or like you are putting her down, even if that isn't your intention.

FINAL WORDS

When you are looking for things to talk about with your girlfriend, you may need to dig far and deep. Often, we like to push past the issues, ignore them, and try to move forward with a positive smile.

That often ends in disaster because, if you don't deal with it head-on, it will come back to get you in the end.

Use these questions and expert advice to make sure you talk to your girlfriend about the questions you should. You will win in the end.

Some Safety Tips When You Are on a First Date

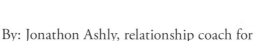

By: Jonathon Ashly, relationship coach for
women, from his relationship blog

I wanted to share some relationship This is stuff that every woman should always know and practice.

Meeting and building quick rapport are so easy online and lately I've noticed that women all too often let their guard down, lose their common sense or abandon their self-protection to a total stranger.

Reflecting on when I was single and looking after my divorce, I'm shocked at how easily a woman **WHO I DID NOT KNOW** would invite me to her home (having never met me before) after a few chats via phone/email/text. It was kind of easy to WOO and WOW women on the phone and they not only thought me to be safe, they felt an almost unique connection with me.

Now I mostly would talk to moms, and the reason for this was I was a dad and believed them safe. Now here is the question, how did they know that I was safe too? They just read a profile about me and maybe read a few correspondences or shared a drink or two at some local bar or a cocktail and lunch at some restaurant now, now this is Doctor Merhish talking I have to say in most cases, I did meet for the first time at over lunch or maybe dinner, by and large most of if not all these women had just met me for the first time. they felt they knew me and felt comfortable with me, and this wasn't true, also felt too. As a man who is an excellent communicator and emotionally connected, I could have been one of the most dangerous of dates, or "Jack" the ripper. Because some women felt instant chemistry and even a spiritual connection with me, as if they had known me all their life "he's different so he must be safe. "I went out with a few, some not, no Chemistry on my side., two or three I dated for a while, and one I am engaged with "And the good news is that I' am safe and so are most guys.

but, is it worth taking the risk for the 1-2% who might be dangerous and worse lose your life?

Trying to provide, here are some common sense safety tips when you think he's different:

I am going to suggest that you always meet in a public place. And yes I would also recommend that you pick-out a place that you like and get to know it, sure more than one if this is your option. And it is true there is safety in numbers. Take a friend, your girlfriend, or sister if you will have one, you just might get a second opinion too. and meeting for the first time in a restaurant or coffee shop would provide enough witnesses should the date turn sour. Never – and I mean never – **meet a man at his home or even think of inviting him to your home until you really get to know him.**

Now How Do You Tell if You Have a Good Man?

By: Dr. Tina Tessina

Ok, taking on Man Picking is one is taking on a real challenge. But for those of you that are looking to try to bring love into your life, please listen to this advice about the real-life qualities, skills and behaviors that help tell us if the guy is really a good guy or not, and has the potential to be a good Partner.

1. **Having Good Judgment**

Good judgment is important because it means you can count on this man to help you make good decisions. You're going to have to make a good number of Judgment calls in a relationship, from something as simple as buying food at the market to buying a home. He will be balanced and think clearly about whatever needs to be done. He is also going to ask you for your opinion if he is going to be a good partner in this relationship. This is what good partners do, it isn't a one man's plan.

When you know your partner has good judgment, you can relax and trust him to do the right thing. If he can trust you, too, then you have the ideal conditions for a working partnership.

Look for: How does he run his life? Does he do well in his own life? Does he handle work well, and take care of his business, pay his bills, make good choices? Is he wise about his money? Pay attention not to how much he sweet-talks you, but to how thoughtful he is about what he does in his life as well as how he treats you.

2. Does he seem intelligent?

Intelligence is important only to a point. There are various kinds of intelligence, and sometimes those who have a lot of academic credits are somewhat lacking in real life, in the good judgment we just discussed. You want someone smart enough to work well with you, and to handle what life hands you as a couple, but academic learning may not be the only way to tell we may have to examine some other areas.

Look for: It's not too difficult to recognize intelligence. But it's important to realize that intelligence is not character. Good judgment and character are more important.

3. Honest, Reliable

What you want is a man who is honest and keeps his promises. This can be as simple as returning a phone call in a timely fashion. Someone who won't do things behind your back (unless it's to buy you a surprise for your birthday) I told my Fiancé that I was going to buy her a small television for the Kitchen a few days ago, and yesterday, we were at Best Buy, and I told her to pick one she liked, and she did. He needs to be Reliability, responsibility and accountability will give him the strength of character he needs to keep his marriage vows and promises.

Dependability and Integrity are very valuable in a marriage, because they mean your relationship will be based on honesty and trust. If there's a problem that makes him dissatisfied in the relationship, he'll be honest enough to tell you, and not just look for instant gratification outside the marriage.

Look for: You can see honesty, dependability and integrity quite easily. How does he handle his business dealings? Can he speak up when something isn't working? Men who cheat are used to taking the easy way out – they want to be liked more than they want to have integrity. Does he feel that he's above the rules? Will he discuss a problem with you until it's solved, or does he walk out? Men who walk out could also go elsewhere when problems arise in the marriage. If he was married before, why did it end? Look at the entire content of his character to see if he'll be faithful.

4. **Affectionate**

Affection is important to women, and often somewhat difficult for men. If your man has trouble showing affection, how will he be as a father? If he equates affection with sex, and cannot be affectionate without expecting sex, you might feel very dissatisfied in the marriage.

Affection and kindness are the lubrication of a relationship. Being able to express positive feelings toward each other helps you get past awkward moments, recover from spats, and reassure each other that your love is still strong. It's also a vital characteristic for both parents to be able to express to their children. Children raised in a combination of affection and discipline grow up secure and with a strong and balanced sense of self. I can't say your man should be like this, but I call my gal, sweetheart all the time, I kiss her, on her head, on the back, hand, and so forth, I and call her sweetheart, honey, my baby, and she is 78 and I am 79, and we are getting together for the first time, and We are getting married soon.

Look for: The key is in his ability to be affectionate in a way that does not inevitably lead to sex. While sex is important, and both of you deserve to have your sexual needs met, a man who pouts if affection doesn't lead to sex is emotionally immature. If he's reluctant to touch, to say loving things, or to be close to you in non-sexual situations, he may have a problem with affection. It's important to talk about it, because he may be concerned about overstepping bounds. But, if he's just repressed in the affection area, your relationship is not likely to do well. Let me share this also, I often will rub down my gals legs, she has as I do too for a matter of fact, have pain in her legs, I have her put her legs over mine as we watch TV, and rub them down with a medicated cream.

There is no "Sex" component, I know that this helps to reduce her pain, and she enjoys the attention, and therapy if you will. The truth is sometimes we share giving each other this kind of attention.

5. Financially Responsible

This is incredibly important, because financial irresponsibility, whether on the part of the woman or the man, will create life-long stress and deprivation. If he gambles money away, spends it on drugs or even just the latest tech toys, or you overspend, the relationship will not work. Running up big debts on credit cards, paying too much for luxury items or houses, lead to problems we can see all around us today.

I believe that a good many folk that marry don't really believe that a marriage or cohabitating relationship is a business as well as a romantic arrangement. Couples are supposed to have income and expenses, and wind up with a profit, which we call savings and equity. Two grown-up partners, who can manage their money well, will be able to create the life they want, support their children, prepare for the future, and have some left over for fun. Good money managers live within their means and are more concerned about whether their purchases are sensible than whether they're fashionable. This very often the "deal breaker", often one of the partners is spending too much money on things, this could very often be clothing, gambling, drinking, and can be a big cause in breaking up the home. Both parties must work together to budget and manage their funds.

Look for: Look at how he's living. Unless he's still a college student, he should have a job, an apartment or house, a car, and some savings and disposable income. You should have the same financial skills. If your relationship is becoming serious, you need to have a discussion where each of you discloses your financial situation with the other. Both of you need a financial plan for your later years and should be able to talk about your shared financial future.

For Where to look for a man, try www.lovefilter.com, Launching today (

The Threat Is Real

If you are over fifty, you need to be extra careful! I believe it is very important that I share this with you. This isn't to say that if you are younger, you do not have to give it some thought. But older people are more likely to have a scam tried on them. I had seven attempted scams during a year and a half. When you lose your money, you likely lose more than younger women. I didn't lose a dime, and one time I got a little hot and took the time to gather information and give it to the police.

The Risk

Once we review this, if it makes you feel that you want to avoid dating online, please don't. Yes, there are some challenges, but with this knowledge, you can be safe. Follow my advice, and you should be fine.

First, remember that in many cases, it's the same way you would act as in the real world. You are not going to give your ID to someone you don't know. And you are not going to give strangers your money, so you should not do this online either.

I am going to assume you are not going to give someone on the street your checkbook and account number, right? This should be the same when you are texting.

If you wouldn't do these things to someone you meet on the street, then you should find it easy to stay safe on the Internet. Continue to use your everyday common sense.

There are two kinds of risks that you might face, so let us take a look.

- A predator online: Someone may try to get some of or all of your savings, your identity, and so on

- A predator in person: You might face the risk of being assaulted sexually by an individual. They could take you out on a date and try to perform this deed.

The greatest risk is the online assault. Your chances of being the target for physical assault is extremely low.

The Upside

Yes, you may be somewhat surprised, but the reward is quite high.

1. High rewards

Scammers have been able to steal hundreds of thousands of dollars from single people. This is a real incentive to one coming from a poverty country.

2. Low risk

The number of online scammers is high because the law doesn't offer a lot of protection in many countries, so the online scammer is at little risk.

3. The scammer has a wide range to cast a net

If you are an in-person kind of criminal, you are going to try to pull your trick on one person at a time. But the online scammer has hundreds, if not thousands, of victims to prey on at one time.

4. It is easy to impersonate someone online

The key to most dating scams is the ability of the scammer to impersonate someone else. The scam often involves some kind of story. One of the gals who tried to scam me started out being very nice to me and wanting to meet me. Then at some point she started talking about being self-employed. She was going to come see me, but she had to change to where she came from. She needed to buy a machine for her business and asked if I could help her. Then she was asking me to send her money. She said,

"I have another friend who also is self-employed and is out of the country on a buying trip. There is problem with funding, and I need to wire her money so she can buy this furniture."

5. If you are older, it is far less likely that you will experience physical assault

There is one piece of good news. If you are a little older, you can expect to not be violated. You should still be careful. That said, if you are in your sixties, you can expect your percentage to be much less than if you are under thirty-five.

If you meet someone for a date, you should be extremely careful, but if you are over fifty, then statistically speaking, then online scams will be your biggest issue.

How to Be Safe

Look them up and be the detective. You need to remind yourself that you know nothing about this person you have just encountered, only what they have told you. You have just met. The good news is that you can find out more, even a great deal. You may learn name, address, family, and more. You can often find people on Facebook.

You can find their friends, information about them, how often they are being contacted and by whom, whether you have mutual friends, and who they say they are. You can find out how many friends they have on other sites.

You can check their posts and see how authentic they are. Are they consistent with the information they tell you?

You can check out their profile and their pictures. This is very simple, using Google for images. As you get information, you follow up this information with a phone call or two. The most important thing that you want to do is gather information that will help keep you safe.

Here Are Some Things Women Do to Protect Themselves

Men do little to protect themselves. But because this is something you can do yourself, it is better that you select a few and try them.

♂	♀
"Nothing. I don't think about it."	"Hold my keys as a potential weapon"
	"Check the backseat before getting in the car"
	"Always carry a cell phone"
	"Don't go jogging at night"
	"Lock the windows when I sleep even on hot nights"
	"Be careful not to drink too much"
	"Never put my drink down & come back to it"
	"Make sure I see my drink being poured"
	"Own a big dog"
	"Carry mace/pepper spray"
	"Have an unlisted number"
	"Have a male voice on my answering machine"
	"Park in well-lit areas"
	"Never use parking garages"
	"Don't get on elevators with a lone man/group of men"
	"Vary my route home from work"
	"Watch what I wear"
	"Don't use highway rest areas"
	"Have & use a home alarm system"
	"Don't wear headphones when jogging"
	"Avoid wooded areas, even in the daytime"
	"Never rent first floor apartments"
	"Only go out in groups"
	"Own a firearm"
	"Always meet men for first dates in public places"
	"Make sure to have cab fare"
	"Never make eye contact with men on the street"
	"Make assertive eye contact with men on the street"
	"Make sure my family knows my itinerary"
	"Have extra locks on my doors & windows"
	"Make sure my garage door is closed all the way before I drive away"
	"Make sure my garage door is closed all the way before I get out of my car"
	"Leave outside lights on all night"
	"Lock my car doors as soon as I get in the car"

You know that old saying "Better safe than sorry"? It is the men who are attacking the women. In 2015, Israeli Prime Minister Goda responded, "If there is going to be a curfew, let the men stay at home." These safety practices have become essential to ensure safety on a daily basis, and they are part of a regular routine. Despite having to go through all of these cautions, we still feel uneasy about going in public and running into issues. Positive efforts have been made to help the uneasy feelings settle, but we can't help it.

Until you've experienced the harassment, catcalls, inappropriate stares, or the feeling of being watched or violated, you simply cannot relate. It is the worst feeling in the world, and you will never be the same afterwards. *What's even more twisted is that society wants to make us seem crazy or feel humiliated for making these precautions after we've felt violated or been harmed.*

It's important that instead of bashing women for protecting themselves in simple ways, that we encourage them to continually proceed with caution and help them in any way you can. We should also become more aware of issues when we see them, such as body language or listening to unwanted conversations. They are a lot more common than you think.

Most importantly, we should be educating young women how to defend themselves, prevent these issues to the best of their abilities, and teach them these safety techniques that we all swear by to prepare themselves for the issues they may face since we apparently can't educate people how to not harass, assault, intimidate or leave women alone.

Men will blame these insecurities or cautionary exercises on the color of their skin, the size or how that person is dressed. **It's not the race of a person or their behaviors that scare women in public; their gender does.** Let's be honest, men scare the hell out of us in public literally all because one dude creeped us out at one point and now their gender is tarnished.

The most important thing that we can and should is to educate our young women how to defend themselves, prevent these issues to the best we can teach you young people the safety techniques we all swear by, preparing themselves for the issues they may face in any given day since we apparently can't educate people how not to harass, assault, intimidate or leave our women alone. I am not just suggesting this to fill up another page in this book, no, I have a daughter myself, and a granddaughter in her twenties also.

Things You Can Do on a Date

Have you wondered what else we might do on a date?

Now, I can't say that I invented these, nor have I done them all, but I will say I am going to introduce them to my gal. We get tired of going to bad movies. We eat out a lot, but often we end up at the same old spots, and we do the same activities. Try one or more of the following and have a good time.

1. If you find yourself in California, Utah, Colorado, or one of the great regions in America, there are woodlands and great outdoor spaces. Take your date on a walk in the park. It can be a short or long walk. Even if you are not really into it, keep strolling. There isn't any set time to take a walk in the park and take advantage of the fresh air.

2. You might think that meeting for breakfast is odd, but if the person you are with is not working out for you, this gives you the rest of the day to meet and spend time with another person. Or if there is a spark, you can keep the date going.

3. Here is something you can do almost any day, indoors or outdoors. Go skating, whether roller or ice. It has been some time for me, but back in Iowa many moons ago, it was a place where we could show off both times of the year.

4. Yes, call me a little nutty, and this may be a little over the top for some and ambitious. But often this is a way to develop a bond: learn some new recipes to try out. Go to an outdoor market or a food fair.

5. If you are adventurous, there is skydiving. If someone is afraid of heights, some practice is required, and now there is a safer way to get a similar experience. They have these places where they offer large wind machines where you learn to fly, but you aren't hundreds of feet in the air. You can try this experience. I guarantee that your date will be impressed.

6. You might find this a little nuts, but you might find it a good idea to adopt a cat or dog. I adopted two dogs at one point, both rescues, and several cats. This can be a big step in a relationship, so really think about it.

7. Have you ever considered meeting for a picnic by a lake or river? Bring along some wine and bread. Now, this really doesn't work for me because I am not a real wine guy, but there are a number of you out there who are, and you might throw in some poetry too. I would enjoy the lake or river, however.

8. As I was doing my research, I found a number of women of varying ages and across the country who were into firing guns at a gun range. It can be done indoors or outdoors, and it just happens to be one of my favorite activities. It can be fun for a number of us, and it can

be tied in with self-defense. Most ranges have training programs for getting a gun license too.

For me, it was great to find women my age who like to shoot and maybe even hunt. I leave this up to you, but I tried tactical training too. To give back to the community, I even hunt wild hogs in Texas. My fiancée and I are both looking to get back to the range, and I want to introduce her to automatic weapon firing.

9.   I can't say I have much experience with this, but many enjoy karaoke. It is something to try rather than going to yet another film.

10. Have you been to a softball game lately? Well, we have. Did you know that there are many cities across the county that have dozens of games going on every week? Many times you are going to find friends and neighbors playing slow-pitch softball. You might find this fun, different, and inexpensive.

11. Feeling adventurous? You don't want to do this with every Tom, Dick, or Harry, but if you have a somewhat close, longtime friend, or maybe you want a double date, be careful if you are going to try this little experiment. There is a lot of this great country to see, with plenty of places to go, so take an overnight trip. We went to an old mining town in Nevada, and there is Silver City. There are also casinos nearly everywhere. A ski or beach trip could work too. This can give you that trip you have been looking for, and maybe it will rekindle some romance you have been missing.

12. Here are two ideas I have never tried. One is taking a cooking class together, and the other is taking a painting class. I took an art class with a younger gal, and yes, it did work out, but I believe you need a lot of commitment from both sides to complete the class. As you may recall, summer classes are shorter.

A Few More Ideas for You!

Water skiing

Hiking

Bowling

Fishing

Handball

Croquet

Snorkeling (may have to take training first)

Beach party for two

Off-roading in a 4×4

Bicycling

Pickle ball

Archery

LGBTQ Dating

We need to take time for the homosexual segment of our society, if we are truly interested in people finding their true love!

It is only fair because they too are trying to find the right person to fulfill their hearts and make them happy. As with a monogamous or heterosexual relationship, there are situations and things that must be considered.

It became the law of the land back in 2015, however most same-sex couples couldn't make their unions officially legal. This means they didn't have the same financial issues as heterosexual couples. Yes, there were issues with getting married.

For one thing, these couples couldn't have a Roth IRA, which had an impact on their financial goals.

Along with these financial goals to consider, there are a few legal documents, some issues with next of kin and family, and decisions to make with marriage on the table. Lesbian and gay couples now face new decisions, with these new financial arrangements and decisions hanging over their heads.

Let's Talk about Tax Issues

I am sorry to start off this way, but your taxes could be one of the biggest changes for you and your mate. This could be positive or negative after you are married. It might be a very good idea that you talk to your income tax person to try to avoid any surprises. As you may know or can assume, there are a number of changes and a few surprises, so you are not alone.

Look at and Discuss Government Benefits

You can find that today that people in same Sex marriages can now qualify for Social Security based on their Spouse's income. This can be a huge change in the law for couples. Especially if one of the partners makes less or more money than the other. You can see a very large benefit and financial gain. Now these benefits vary Sometimes we will see some Lesbians, couples getting married just for the benefits, then again, you can find the other extreme, when the couples see no rush to get married, but they treat each other caring couples. They often want to get married because it is the right thing to do, not for money, but because it is the right thing to do.

The following information comes from Emily Starbuck Crone, staff writer at NerdWallet.

- **<u>Getting Health Insurance</u>**
  Most of us are aware that most employer's health Insurance plans offer spousal coverage. If you or your partner has a generous health care plan, getting married on the same plan can mean a savings in premiums to the couple.

- **<u>Determine financial aid needs</u>**
  If the couple has a child

  If you are both legal, have a child, and parent, the income of both parents must be reported to the FAFSA – Application for financial aid for higher Education responsibility – regardless of the marital status. But if by chance you are unmarried and just one partner is the legal partner, only this partner is the legal partner, this partner's income is required. If you are in this situation, This situation could potentially put your child at a disadvantage for obtaining financial aid or a need-based award.

  It just happens that the same thing happens if your partner or are married, and your partner is in school or is planning to go back to school using aid or a Scholarship. This means you can't hear those wedding bells, but, as you know, each one of you couples are different, and your situations are different, so it can make sense financially to put off the big wedding until you finish school, but it is in your corner to make this decision.

  Now this is the same situation that same sex couples, much discuss, and think about......

- **Receiving money or gifts**
  Oh yes, if you are a legal spouse, you can give money or gifts to one another "freely", but exceeding $14,000 per person, in 2017 according to the IRS. And at the same time, it is suggested getting caught is suggested is highly rare, but it can be a real nightmare. And if you are unmarried, and just happen to pass away, with a large Estate, that you are leaving to a your partner in a will it is very possible that your partner will have to pay an Estate tax or inheritance tax, depending on where you live.

- There is another way!
  Yes, <u>consider </u>domestic partnerships instead. "Now the only way you can get the 1,138 federal rights and responsibilities that are associated with Marriage.

  But if you believe that marriage would be harmful to your finances you could enter into a domestic partnership instead. And you will find that there are various kinds, plus those provided by State and local governments, as well by some employers, nationwide. So my advice to you is seek out information first before you do anything, and select the best situation that fits your needs.

- Most important don't rush
  Yes, for most of us, getting married can be fun and exciting. Plus, for many it may be financially beneficial too. But at the same time it is highly irresponsible if one or both of you are not ready.

Reasons Why Relationships Break Up

If any of these reasons show up, it is time to say adios.

Bad Habits. It may have been okay to have been an outlaw when you were young and playing games. But if you can't do it on your own, find some help and clean it up. And start now before you find someone and start a new relationship.

Cheating. So you have been breaking the law of the land and the vows of God. Regardless of whether you were married, you have given up your personal integrity, broken a few hearts, and lost your honor. If you give up the idea of having sex with others, you will find that your mate will start looking better to you.

Misdirected Anger. I am sure that you can identify times that you have had trouble at work or on the road, and you came home in a terrible mood and took it out on your spouse. This type of behavior is unfair. Over time this misdirected anger is going to have a bad effect on your relationship with your spouse. This kind of action will bring only negative energy and can make things worse. You need to change, even if it means just giving your spouse a hug or kiss. In fact, I always say, "Happy wife, happy life." Just this morning, I was saying this to my wife, Francie. Every morning as I walk by her, I give her a kiss or hug.

Being Unsupportive. If you can't be supportive to the one you love when he or she is down or stressed, you are not worth your spouse's time or energy. What you are saying to your loved one is that she or he is not worth your time, and you don't care. This kind of behavior is saying, I don't want to be here for you, and it is time for you to be gone.

Toxicity. This wasn't a big thing in our case, but if in your case if you have one or more friends whom your partner can't stand, whether it is a control thing or these people have negative things going on, it needs addressing.

In our situation, we do have one thing going on, but in this case there is a real issue we both are involved in, and you could have such a situation as well. If you have a negative person in both of your lives, that person should not be there. If this person engages in bad behavior, he or she should not be in your and your partner's lives. You also need to find other people to hang out with. This is true if this person engages in bad behavior or is disrespectful of your partner or mate.

Lying. So you think you have to lie because you are doing something that would make you look bad in the eyes of your partner. Give up the dishonesty, and your relationship can change for the better, often quickly. But keep up the lying, and you can lose all trust that your partner had in you.

Stealing. I must share that financial issues account for over 30 percent of divorce among couples. This financial infidelity suggests that if you are going to steal from someone you are supposed to love, you have major issues and need professional help. If you feel that you are entitled to these funds, you still need help and counseling. If you can't work out these feelings, you may as well say goodbye and move along.

Giving Up. The couple that does the work and faces the challenges of the day will stand the test of time. Giving up is the same as giving in, which is the process that needs to be considered when you are at odds with one another. You don't have to agree with your mate on everything; you can agree to disagree and move along.

Not Communicating. Giving up is not the same as giving in, and silence is never golden. Yes, the most important thing in any relationship is communication. The more you talk, the better you will feel. If you don't have good communications, you can't have a good relationship. So here is the plan: Sit down close together over a cold drink or a cup of coffee. Use simple words. You will find that you will get more communication out of this process.

You may be surprised that simply sitting down and changing how you relate is as simple as eliminating a bad habit. However, you may have to seek outside help.

If you really want to stay together, you may be required to look at any of these behaviors and why.

In a Relationship, There Are Things That You Should Never Have to Feel

Whether it is a new relationship or one that has been around for some time, you need to know that it is not unusual to have high and low emotions at times. However, these swings should only go to certain levels. There are certain things that you should never feel in your relationship. If you do, they can greatly damage it. These things include a lack of communication, a lack of satisfaction, and a misbalance between you and your partner. Unless these feelings are resolved, you will find that they lead to conflict, or even the break of a long-term relationship.

Often couples feel happy, accepted, and loved in their relationship. Many have their bouts with sadness or rage, and disappointments, but most of the time the overall experience is positive. One's overall experience should never be negative. Change this through proper, meaningful dialogue. It might be the time for you and your partner to evaluate the relationship to determine whether this relationship is the right one for both of you. There are a number of feelings that could come up that may suggest you should seek a different situation—and fast.

- If you feel that the relationship is one-sided, this should be a clue that it isn't someplace you should be.
- If you find that this relationship seems like a lot of work, there is a good chance that you should move on.
- If you are feeling unappreciated, you need to evaluate being in this relationship. If you find that you are not appreciated and are taken for granted, it is time to find someone who doesn't take you for granted.
- If you have the feeling that you are ashamed of yourself, you need to work out the differences with your partner. You should never

feel ashamed of yourself in any relationship. It is not worth your time or energy to be in this type of negative relationship.

- Having the feeling that your partner is not with you. When you are together, the both of you should have a good connection and feel as if you enjoy being with each other. But if your partner seems like he or she is in the other room or is on the phone, ignoring you, then if you can't work it out, you may need to find greener pastures.

Here are more things you should not have to experience in your relationship.

Feeling anxious around your partner

You should never feel anxious around your partner. You will find that this is emotional abuse. That is not the right person for you. What you should feel is excitement and happiness, not sadness and worry. This should be a happy experience for the both of you.

Feeling like you are being forced to have sex

You should never have sex with anyone whom you do not want, or when you are not in the mood—even in a relationship. This is rape, and it is a real sign that something is wrong. Your relationship should not be based upon sex. This abusive partner may say things like, "Other women are doing this. What is wrong with you?"

Feeling that you are constantly being corrected or criticized

If your partner is constantly correcting you and criticizing you, you don't need this abuse. It is time to have a real discussion about this treatment. If it isn't corrected, it is time to find another partner. Remember that this kind of treatment should never be tolerated.

Feeling that your partner isn't present with you

If you are together, you both should have a good relationship and conversations, as well be each other's center of attention. Enjoy each other. If your partner is on the phone and ignoring you, making you feel bad, then in my opinion you are in the wrong relationship.

Feeling like the relationship is one-sided

You should never feel the relationship is one-sided. It if feels like work and a lot of effort goes into this relationship to try to make it successful and suitable, then over time, people may change and grow together. But if your relationship feels like too much work or a chore, this is likely not the relationship for you. It may be hard to break up, but having a relationship should not feel like a chore. It might be better to hit the road now rather than later.

Feeling Unappreciated

If this is how you feel, it is a good time to take a good, long look. Evaluate your relationship and decide what the next steps should be. If you feel that you are always taken for granted and the other person doesn't appreciate your contributions to the relationship, then you should reevaluate why you are in this relationship in the first place.

Feeling that you have been deceived

If you think that your partner is deceiving you or lying to you all the time, this could indicate that he or she has a trust problem and possibly other issues that can cause problems in the relationship. You likely need to step back and review whether you should continue in this commitment.

Let's Review Some Points to Remember

I would like you to be clear as to why you want to find someone to be with and love again. Is it because you want someone to help you pay the bills? Let's be honest here. Or do you really enjoy the company of a loving person? Do you really enjoy the feeling and glow inside? I have to say when I lost my second wife, I could feel a piece of my heart being taken away from me. At the time, I wasn't looking to get married again, but I was looking for a special person whom I could be with and go out to dinner with. I did have my two dogs, but it wasn't the same thing.

I didn't have a favorite bar to hang out at. I sat by myself with the dogs, and I found that less than appealing. I didn't have that big of a hobby to launch into. My kids were not that close, and they were in other states. I do have a good-sized family, if there was greater interest, but the distance limited visits with most of the family. I did enjoy having someone to share my life with, but I did not have a big "belong to that gang" mentality.

My first approach was to start getting involved in dating sites, and I found it very challenging, somewhat demanding, and much different than the dating I had experienced twenty-three years earlier. I felt unsatisfied, disappointed, and frustrated. But I decided to make it work for me, and I pushed forward.

At one point, I wanted it to work for me, and then the research part of it developed. I tried to help others if I could.

By and large, we know that older gentlemen are more experienced because they have faced the challenges of time, and they are often more cultured. Younger men are more into themselves and more apt to play more. They are also less reliable.

It makes sense that older guys are more financially stable. Young men are in training mode and are testing the waters to determine which career they would like to pursue. They may be going to school.

I am going to generalize a bit here, but older gentlemen are more likely to be seeking a serious relationship, whereas younger guys want to play. You will find that the more senior man wants to please his woman. As a rule, the older guy has more sophisticated taste. Yes, he is done drinking out of a hose.

Older guys are usually better cooks, though take this statement with a grain of salt. Yes, I can cook, and I boil water with a little help, but with the gal I am with, I am somewhat at a loss at cooking. This skill is going to vary with the gentleman, but the younger guy is more satisfied with Whataburger.

You can expect the older gentleman to be more respected for his healthy lifestyle, whereas the younger guy is often not so healthy. Yes, there was a time where I could work all day, eat glass, spit bullets, and dance all night. But not today. And you are not going to find us going ninety-five miles per hour down the freeway with you on the back or our motorcycle.

If you still enjoy going out partying, you might enjoy the lifestyle of the younger guy, but as a rule you will find the older gentleman is unlikely to go out partying as often as the younger guy. However, I had a serious relationship with a young woman back in Burlingame, California, and often one could find her on the bed passed out, whereas I was bright-eyed and bushy-tailed. I simply didn't enjoy partying that hard. You have a choice here.

To change the subject somewhat, be careful in a group situation, such as on a cruise ship, in a party, or at a club. We can see abduction, trafficking, and more. You can become a victim, and you can become secretly drugged.

Here are some things that a "real" man does when he is in a relationship. If you are in a relationship and do not enjoy these things, you need to take a long, hard look at what is going on. Then decide whether you would like to continue in this manner.

1. A real man loves and respects his woman for who she is. He might not love her all the time, but Unlike those guys whose intentions are to fool around and not fully commit to their **relationship, real men** genuinely commit to a **relationship**
2. A real man commits to the relationship fully. He doesn't cheat. He is loyal to his partner and knows …
3. A real man protects his partner physically and emotionally. Not that a woman can't protect herself.
4. A real man fulfills his partner mentally and sexually. This may not be all the time, but he is there
5. A **real man** commits to the **relationship** fully. Unlike those guys whose intentions are to fool around and not fully commit to their **relationship, real men** genuinely commit to a **relationship**. They proudly introduce their partners to the important people in their lives. They will not hide their beloved.

Here are three reasons why women prefer younger guys. You must choose wisely when choosing a partner. Much of it is based on more emotion than logic, and perhaps that is why we have a lot of divorce.

Older men are often already married. You will find that this is the most common reason **why** older **women** seek **younger men**. They are going to find a lack of **choice** at their age, which makes them search below their age—and that often turns out well. This may sound somewhat over the top, but you older gals like younger men because they can take the lead in the bedroom. There is a different energy level, and younger guys can stay in the game.

Your job is to analyze the objectives, and based upon your wants and needs, make the best selection you can on your behalf. Here is some food for thought: the rule is you should select a man at least five years your senior to have the best results.

Be yourself and have an open mind. As I suggested early on, take defense training. You are not doing this for me—I am talking about your life and your protection. I don't want to scare or offend you, but consider a firearms class.

Always be ready for awkward moments. Before you start the process of dating, do it for the right reasons.

Don't play games. Remember that the other person has a heart too!

Have fun and make sure it is a good fit

Play it safe at all times.

Don't give up on your own goals.

Know when to say goodbye.

Again, this is not a game!

Isn't how long you spend together that counts as you develop your relationship—it's the quality of time. It's about how honest you are with yourself and your partner. I was married the first time after about three months of dating, and we were honest to each other and ourselves. I was about twenty-four years old, and she was about twenty-seven. We were married, and I have to say that her family was very supportive. We agreed on the same goals and discussed them often. Looking back, I would more than likely, change them slightly. I would have agreed on more children; we had two. We were married for over twenty-eight years. You need to work together and stay on the same train. I must admit that I was not as patient, and I tried to improve my career quickly—sometimes too quickly. Maybe I took too many risks and did not think of the other person as I should have. Of course, this is Monday morning quarterbacking and a little too late, but it is food for thought.

As an example, I started a small toy company in California. This didn't go well. We had a good little product, and it started off okay, but the federal government banned not our product but that of a larger firm for safety reasons. Ours was safer and more attractive, but they looked similar in many ways. We moved in the eighties for family reasons, and I had some issues getting a job, but I was subbing and got a sales position. I did this for a while, but then I got into the oil industry, which started to grow.

But before I could say, "My name is Jack Roberson," the oil business tanked, and the big firms were selling their equipment off for ten cents on the dollar. We didn't have issues with inventory, but we still had rent to pay and salaries. I discovered that one of my employees was stealing, and I had to deal with that too. Again I had to close the business, and the employee went to jail.

We moved many times. Sure, we discussed it, but looking back, maybe we should have spent more time looking at our options.

In any event, my first wife decided to leave me during year twenty-eight, and she left about two years later but did not complete the divorce. I did this after she moved away.

At the same time, I lost my new home, my new car, and my sales and marketing manager position. I had been working in sales and marketing as well as education. We had moved back and forth, from California, to Utah, Idaho, and back. Did this contribute to the breakup? Looking back, I think so, as did my off-and-on career. Hopefully you can learn from the mistakes of others.

This loss of employment put a real hardship on me. I was job searching, and I vowed to not give up and reestablish a relationship. I knew I enjoyed being married, so I started looking for someone. This was not an easy task. The dating game was not the same, and we were just getting into computers. There were dating tabloids and newspaper ads. We used the phone, wrote to each other using a typewriter (a device that you may not be that familiar with), and of course used the computer. We used the phone a lot.

I was living in an apartment in Southern California. I would answer the clips in the newspaper and tabloids. Some came with pictures, but some did not. I also tried to answer the ads that were close to where I was. I had been in the area for maybe five years, but it was so vast that I didn't know it well. In those days, we had a large book with addresses and such, but it was page after page of road maps. The other big consideration was the drive.

After dating women from all over the area—Los Angeles, Riverside, and San Bernardino—I often had to budget my funds. Sometimes I didn't know whether I had money for gas and dinner, and I was not sure I was going to get back from this date. I have to say I met a good number of women, some attractive and some not so much. Some were a little nuts. I met one I really liked, and I thought we had something. I was still working at finding and keeping a job. I got one and was developing it, and after a few weeks, I was fired. I ran out of money, so I called "Sandy" to tell her about it. She broke up with me in the next few days. We would go out dancing and sing to each other. I believed that I had something going on.

One time I met a doctor in Los Angeles, but this didn't last long. I wanted more, but I believe I was below her economically. Plus, we lived more than fifty miles apart.

I dated this cute airline hostess. We went to a movie and were standing in the line to go in. As some folks passed us, I reached up and touched her waist to move her from bumping into the people passing by. She screamed at me, "Don't touch me!" After I took her home, that was the last date with her.

Did I have some enjoyable dates? Yes, very much so. I moved in with a gal. For a while, I was going with a sex therapist, for a few weeks, and she might have taught me a few things I didn't know. I can't remember why we stopped seeing each other. We would go for walks in her area, and she was nice looking. She had no family or kids at home.

Eventually, I met my second wife. She was a divorced nurse and had two girls. We got along great. I was fighting to survive, and we did have some challenges with one of our children. I was teaching part-time here and there at some high schools and a few junior colleges. It seemed that my luck had changed when I got a full-time job teaching. I was teaching at some junior colleges and adult education classes. One of the classes was based on my first book, *Jump Start Your Career*. I got a chance to go to China to teach a business marketing class to Chinese graduate students. The school paid for my trip, and for doing the class.

Bobbie and I moved to a retirement home in Corona, California. Along the way, Bobbie got interested in raising alpacas, so we started our own herd. We leased land with another alpaca rancher and took classes together. We later moved to Denton, Texas, and bought a retirement home there near her oldest daughter's family so she could talk to them nearly every day. She even went back to work in case management, but not as a director.

Then she got cancer and went south, and I lost her three and a half years later. We did have twenty-three years together. We didn't agree on everything. She would have her glass of wine at dinner, and I might have my beer. I went shooting at the range and sometimes hunted pigs. She visited her daughter. We had family dinners too. I was and still am very close to both my son-in-law and my daughter-in-law. I'm not so close to my own kids. I would have liked to have had a bigger family.

Now, things have changed. I met my fiancée during the research of this subject. I was going into a depression because my wife's cancer hit me hard, and the loss was harder. I was going from two depression pills a day to four. I joined dating sights and moved from my very nice home in Denton, Texas, to a smaller place. When I started dating, I was very disappointed. It wasn't because the gals were not attractive, although as they say, beauty is in the eye of the beholder. But I found that a lot of the women were not sure why they were on the site. It seemed that they as a group wanted to talk more—not face-to-face but on the computer. When I was dating, I was meeting more than 80 percent of the women I asked out the first time, but my rate for a second date was around 10 percent. You must remember I didn't start out to write a book on this subject, so I was not collecting information at that time.

I have had two guy friends for several years. I lived just down the street from Vern, and our families were close. Jack and I worked together, and I wrote and called him for years. Vern is my age, and Jack is in his late sixties. Independently, they realized that I was having some issues, so they got after me to write a book, knowing that I had done the first four.

Of course, I said I had no idea what to write about. Sure I was an educator and teacher, but this wasn't a big part of me, and it had been some time. But here we are.

Then of course, a year ago, I got cancer, and I have been fighting this prognosis. I had my forty-five radiation treatments, I have my major examination in October this year, and I am hopeful I will get my testosterone back in October or December of this year.

Moving in Together

One of the most hectic days of your life will be moving in together. Sure, you may have moved before, but have you moved two households into one? Well, hello, Goodwill! I have to tell you I recently moved my stuff from a home I had been in for two years, but I also moved my belongings from a much larger home, and for a long time there were two people's belongings everywhere, with furniture to boot. She had been in her place for about twelve years and wanted to keep many of her things. I had stuff too—family pictures, and some very nice wood pieces. I am not a real Western guy, but I had a number of Western items, pictures, and rugs. It was suggested to me that she didn't want these items, so much went off to Goodwill also. As for my family and career pictures, they may not go up on walls because there is no room. I can keep my kids' pictures in a box, along with my first and second wives' pictures. This was a little hard for me. I also had some weapons pictures that I had collected. I gave many to Goodwill, a few will go into my office, and the rest will go into boxes in the attic.

If you are older, you will know what I mean. This is my eighteenth house. As you get older, the moves get more difficult. Of course, you may already know this. There is stress about deciding what to take, where to put it, and what to give away. We had decided that there were two old pieces that were at her place, and they were to go to her son's place. We carefully put them in my new truck, but on the way over, they "jumped" out of my truck and exploded in the street, with the traffic around us seemingly trying to run over me and the folks helping pick up the pieces. One cabinet was completely destroyed, but the other not so much. We got the good one in, and about five blocks down the road, it jumped out again. This time it was dead. Some folks were not too happy. I was disappointed.

This is not the only stress area. It can be an everyday occurrence. Why am I telling this story? We are in these situations all the time. You are going to get a different look at your partner. Is this the person you want to be with for the rest of your life? Is this a deal breaker? This may not be on your list, but I wanted to warn you.

I must tell you that as far as I am concerned, moving will always be a stressful activity, just like bills, children, mothers-in-law, and other members of the family. This could be a deal breaker before you tie the knot. For some of you, it may be hard to get over giving up or storing your valuable moments. I share this with you because this is something you and your partner should discuss. Reach an agreement about what stays, what goes, and where it goes. I tried to give some of our family photos to my children, but there was little to no interest. Someday, I am sure, some of my children or grandkids will have an interest, but they will be gone.

The Most Hectic Day of Your Life

Your wedding day is the most hectic day of your life. It also sets the tone of your life together.

You will find there is a lot of help out there, with apps to help you plan your wedding. You are not going to have to carry a wedding binder around with you, so that relieves stress already.

Wedding apps help reduce the time you spend on things, and they keep your wedding organized and running well.

I am going to assume that you have a budget, and of course you would like to stick to it or at least be close. There are good social networks out there that will help you save time and money by offering a large selection of wedding items, and there are bridal magazines that review things. Very often women will spend time searching these magazines for that dream wedding dress. Often you will find that bridal magazines simply don't have the variety to meet your wedding needs.

More than likely your wedding day will be the most hectic day of your life. I found myself going around in a daze. In fact, I lost my shoes. We found them, but as I recall, my best man had to drive back to my new father-in-law's house to retrieve them. This isn't to say that my new bride wasn't amazing. Even if you are stressed out, often later you will break out in laughter about the stories for years to come.

This is not to say that is all there is. You should have a wedding registry, organize guests and seating, and more. I wish you good luck and a happy future.

Now, I hope this book can provide you with a little help along the way to some happiness!

THE AUTHOR

Dr. Ferris E. Merhish, known to friends as Gene, is an instructor for colleges, adult education programs, and high schools with more than eighteen years of teaching experience. He is trained in business education, distributive education, and marketing and sales, and he has experience as an entrepreneur. He was recognized as a business education consultant for the State of California. Several years ago, he operated one of the most advanced programs in the teaching or retail merchandising industry in the western states. Also, he has been a department chair in a Southern California high school, where he has also been teaching computer technology; he wrote a training workbook for the course.

In addition, Dr. Merhish has over twenty-six years of business and marketing experience with such firms as Proctor and Gamble, Gardner-Denver, and Harnischfeger Corporation. He has created and operated at least two entrepreneurial companies. He has served as a business and marketing (adjunct) instructor for Ivy University in Alhambra, Riverside Community College, Chaffey Community College in Rancho Cucamonga, and others. He also worked in the consort with the China Training Center for Senior Civil Servants, the Ministry of Personnel, the People's Republic of China, Orange County Juvenile Hall, and Job Corps. Furthermore, Dr. Merhish works with small businesses as a marketing and sales consultant. This will be Dr. Mehrieh's fourth book published; his first book was *7001 Resumes*, and his third book was *7001 Resumes—Plus, Second Edition*.

This book is based on direct research and experience as a widower seeking an opportunity to find a new companion, move forward into the sunset of his life, and find love and happiness with his new companion.

I would like to thank the following individuals for their help in contributing to this book.

> Mary Stevenson, Dallas, Texas
> Jack Worthington, Ogden, Utah
> Vern Thomason, Phoenix, Arizona
> Bri Rhoades, Keller, Texas

I also would like to thank these longtime friends who were instrumental in getting me writing again. I am not sure whether they felt I had something to contribute or were simply trying to keep me busy.

Printed in the United States
by Baker & Taylor Publisher Services